Clara in Blunderland

BEWARE THE PORLOCROCK, MY JOE! (*PAGE 18*)

Clara
in Blunderland

A political parody based on
Lewis Carroll's Wonderland

by Caroline Lewis

ILLUSTRATIONS BY
J. STAFFORD RANSOME

evertype

2010

Published by Evertype, Cnoc Sceichín, Leac an Anfa, Cathair na Mart, Co. Mhaigh Eo, Éire. *www.evertype.com*.

This edition © 2010 Michael Everson.

First edition London: William Heinemann, 1902.

A catalogue record for this book is available from the British Library.

ISBN-10 1-904808-49-2
ISBN-13 978-1-904808-49-7

Typeset in De Vinne Text, Mona Lisa, ENGRAVERS' ROMAN, and *Liberty* by Michael Everson.

Illustrations: J. Stafford Ransome, 1902.

Cover: Michael Everson.

Printed by LightningSource.

Foreword

*C*aroline Lewis is a pen-name, that of the team of Edward Harold Begbie (1871–1929), J. Stafford Ransome (born 1860), and M. H. Temple, who wrote both *Clara in Blunderland* and a sequel, *Lost in Blunderland*. These two novels deal with British frustration and anger about the Boer War and with Britain's political leadership at the time. Much of Begbie's work was as a journalist, though he also wrote non-fiction, biographies, and some twenty-five novels, ranging from children's stories to explorations of personal psychology and spirituality. In 1917, he publicly agreed with the pacifists in their opposition to the war and defended the right of conscientious objectors not to fight in it. Later he wrote some of his best-known investigative and satirical work under the pen-name "A Gentleman with a Duster".

J. Stafford Ransome, the illustrator of both *Blunderland* books, also worked as a journalist. Moreover he wrote on such wide-ranging subjects as labour relations, engineering in South Africa, and woodworking machinery.

In 1902 M. H. Temple collaborated again with Begbie and Ransome in *The Coronation Nonsense Book* (in the style of Edward Lear). Previously in 1894 he contributed satirical political verse to *The Hawarden Horace* by Charles L. Graves.

I should make it clear that I am not a student of early twentieth-century British politics—but I'm not publishing this book because of its value to the study of that time and place. I'm publishing it because it's a splendid parody, amusing both for what it parodies as for its reflection of Carroll's original.

It is by no means my intention to annotate this edition, but I can—with the help of a review in the British Empire League's periodical *United Australia* ("One people one destiny")*—give some guidance to the reader. In the section "Literary Note and Books of the Month", Evelyn Dickinson, writes from London:

> *Clara in Blunderland*, by Caroline Lewis, (Heinemann, 6s.).
> A small volume of capital fooling. Caroline Lewis has kept as closely as possible to the lines of Lewis Carroll, and "S. R." has wrought as much as possible like Sir John Tenniel, so that familiar echoes and resemblances pursue us all the while we read. "Clara" is Mr Balfour; "Blunderland" is the politics of the moment, wherein play the Red Queen (Mr Chamberlain); the Duchess (Lord Salisbury), who is also referred to by Clara as "Aunt Sarum"; Crumpty-Bumpty (Mr Campbell-Bannerman); the Walrus (Sir William Harcourt); the Dalmeny Cat (Lord Rosebery); and various other prominent statesmen. Many a true word is spoken here in jest.

Biographical summaries (to 1902) and photos will certainly help the reader to put the cartoon parodies into context, and guide the reader who wishes to pursue an interest in any of these characters, or in the ramifications of the Second Boer War in general.

---

* Vol. II, No. 12, 20 June 1902

Clara: Arthur Balfour (1848–1930), Member of Parliament for Manchester East, was First Lord of the Treasury and Leader of the House of Commons during Lord Salisbury's adminstration from 1895–1900. *Clara in Blunderland* was written *before* Balfour became Prime Minister in 1902 on Lord Salisbury's resignation.

The Red Queen: Joseph Chamberlain (1836–1914) was Secretary of State for the Colonies from 1895 to 1903. In 1899, with British public opinion in favour of military support for the "Uitlanders", he pressed for troop reinforcements to be sent to South Africa. As a result the Boer republics of the Transvaal and the Orange Free State declared war on Great Britain.

The Duchess ("Aunt Sarum"): Robert Cecil, 3rd Marquess of Salisbury (1830–1903) was Prime Minister from 1895 to 1902, serving as Foreign Secretary at the same time. Arthur Balfour was his nephew. The Fashoda crisis occurred during his premiership, and more importantly the Second Boer War (1899–1902). (*Sarum* was the ecclesiastical name of the diocese of Salisbury from the 11th century to the Reformation.)

Crumpty-Bumpty: Sir Henry Campbell-Bannerman (1836–1908) became leader of the Liberals in the House of Commons in 1898. The Boer War (1899–1902) had split the Liberal party into Imperialist and Pro-Boer camps and the party was defeated in the "khaki election" of 1900.

The Walrus: Sir William Vernon Harcourt (1827–1904) was leader of the Liberal Party before Sir Henry Campbell-Bannerman. In 1898 he retired from the party, but as an independent in the years 1899–1900 he vigorously attacked the Conservative government's financial policy and attitude towards the Transvaal.

The Dalmeny Cat: Archibald Philip Primrose, 5th Earl of Rosebery (1847–1929) was Prime Minister from 1894 to 1895. He was in favour of the Boer War and was against Home Rule for Ireland. His opposition to this latter policy meant that he could not participate in the Liberal Government of 1905.

The Caterpillar: Winston Churchill (1874–1965) was captured while a war correspondent for the *Morning Post* during the the Second Boer War. After escaping from a POW camp and returning to Britain in 1900, he published two volumes on his Boer war experiences, *London to Ladysmith via Pretoria* and *Ian Hamilton's March*.

In the end, in 2010, *Clara in Blunderland* has to stand on its own in a way that it didn't in 1902. In my opinion it survives the passage of a century surprisingly well. Politics and politicians haven't changed much, it seems, in a century. That may be regrettable—but at least Caroline Lewis can still make us laugh about it!

Michael Everson
Westport 2010

Dedication to the 1902 Edition

Dedicated
with the most profound affection
and respect to the memory of
Lewis Carroll,
to whom the author is as much
indebted for the text
as the illustrator to Sir John Tenniel
for the ensuing parodies
of his perfect pictures.

Also
with the publisher's courteous
acknowledgement to
Messrs Macmillan,
the godfathers of the original
Alice.

Clara in Blunderland

Contents

DRIFTING

All o'er the sea of Politics
    Full leisurely we glide;
And Britain's bark, with little skill,
    And little care we guide,
While little minds make little plans,
    And stronger hands are tied.

Ah, cruel fate, to make us tell
    This very plaintive story,
Of Clara's trip to Blunderland,
    Of creatures bold and boery;
And clothe in garb of fantasy
    Prosaic Whig and Tory.

A sense of Duty urged us first
  To "hurry and begin it."
Futility then whispered low,
  "It wo'n't take half a minute!"
We laughed to scorn the bare idea
  That there was money in it.

So far we have confined our words
  To merely pointless chatter,
As flat as other prefaces,
  Perhaps a trifle flatter;
But, as the reader always skips
  This part, it does not matter.

One serious word—we have to pay
  Our tribute to those sages
Who wrote and drew that "Wonderland"
  On which are based these pages.
A classic which in nursery land
  Will stand the test of ages.

We claim that naught within these leaves
  Has been set down in malice,
That certainly against the State
  By us there no cabal is—
And, reader, if you've praise to give,
  Bestow it all on Alice.

Chapter I

In a Hole again

*C*lara felt very listless and stupid that afternoon. You see, she had so many governesses and they taught her such very dull lessons. There was Miss Bowles, who tried to instruct her in facts and figures, and all sorts of stupid things of that kind, and Miss Yerburgh, who wanted her to learn about China and other places in which she never could feel any interest, and another lady to teach her the use of the *Globe*; but nobody to give her nice little lessons in kindergarten philosophy, or even to help her and her sister Geraldine in making Irish stew.

No wonder she felt dull; and there was no occasion for surprise when, purely in search of distraction, she went right into a hole on the putting green to

fetch out her ball. People do and say such funny things when they are bored at golf.

You may think it wonderful that such a big girl as Clara could get down a hole of this sort, but she had a marvellous gift in that way, and it was said that she could get into a hole when no one else would have found it possible; so you see she had no difficulty about it.

This particular hole, however, appeared to be bottomless, and the moment she got into it she began to fall, which made her say at once to herself, "Dear me! I must be dreaming again, for of course in real life I could never fall at all. My Aunt Sarum would not allow it."

> But she fell,
> and fell,
> and fell.
> Down,
> down,
> down,

until she began to fear that she would fall right down to the level of the Aberrationals, and come out in Ireland, Where the inhabitants are all cannibals, and the resources of civilization have long ago been exhausted.

"I *do* wish," she said, as she was falling, "I had Geraldine with me. Then I could hide in some Cabinet or other where I should never be noticed and, perhaps, when the Aberrationals had eaten her, they wouldn't be hungry for me. I never knew anybody except Auntie for whom one of the family was not *quite* enough."

She was, so she thought, years and years in falling, and once she nearly saved herself by catching hold of an Old Age Pension which was sticking out of a pigeon-hole in the wall, with nobody to look after it. But it pulled itself back and hissed at her, "just," as she said afterwards, "like a Snake in the Grass." So you see it only caused her to slacken in her downward career for the moment.

A little later she saw in another recess a large and very dusty jar labelled PROGRAMME. She snatched it off the shelf eagerly, as she passed, for she was hungry by this time. "This ought to be good," she said to herself; but, alas! it was empty, and with a sigh she placed it on a lower shelf.

And still she went
down,
down,
down.

At last, however, the great fall was over, and Clara found that she was not nearly so much hurt as she expected.

She found herself sitting on a nice little seat which was as safe as you can imagine, and which was situated in a large hall full of green chairs. In the highest of these sat a very sedate White Rabbit, who said, "Order! Order!" in a loud voice; but as nobody brought any refreshments, and as he said he was "now going to read the bill," Clara thought she had better try to find some way out, as she did not wish to pay for food she had not had.

All the doors were locked, but through the key-hole of one (which bore the inscription "Noblesse Oblige. Admittance £20,000 a year. Liberal discount to Successful Brewers and Unsuccessful Generals.") she could see a beautiful garden, carpeted with flowers of hereditary intellect, and filled with hundreds upon hundreds of happy children, of whom three formed a quorum, and of whom some seemed to be more than half awake. "I shall call that the Palace of Sleeping Beauties," cried Clara, in ecstasies, quite forgetting that a garden ca'n't be a palace.

She tried very hard to get through the key-hole into this charming place, but it was of no use, and when she found that she would have to stop in the hall with the green chairs and

hear the White Rabbit read the bill, she sat down and cried
and cried.

"Must I stop here for ever and ever?" she moaned.

"My dear," answered the White Rabbit, "I am afraid you
will never leave this house until it is dissolved."

"Oh dear, oh dear," she said, despairingly. "Why *was* it built
on such solid foundations?"

"You ought to be very thankful," he added, "after your great
come down, to be here at all when you think how many strange
creatures are trying to get in and ca'n't."

After the bill was read the serious business began. The hall
became full of all sorts of animals. "Both quadrangles and
biceps," as she told Geraldine afterwards. There were a good
many geese, a very ugly duckling, some saucy monkeys, wolves
in sheeps' clothing, parrots in eagles' feathers, guinea pigs
looking about for guineas, pigeons, cuckoos, and any quantity
of rats. These strangely assorted creatures began at once to

wrangle, and insult each other, and soon there was a free fight, which lasted, Clara could not say how long.

At length, however, the White Rabbit rose from his seat, and pulled out his Watch, crying, "Time! Time!"

Then the animals and birds trooped out of the hall, and Clara found herself hustled by the crowd out into the lobby.

When the noisy party had thinned down somewhat, a stately Dodo approached Clara diplomatically, and said politely, "I have been watching you for some time in the house, and, if you will excuse my saying so, my dear, admiring your way of looking on while other people did the business. It seems to me that you have grasped the meaning of that policy of masterly inactivity which is the key-note to our Party Tactics."

Clara did not understand the meaning of all these long words, but she smiled prettily.

"You are still a comparatively innocent child," continued the Dodo, with kindly patronage, "and what you want is Protection."

"I do wear a chest protector in the winter," said Clara, "and I don't like it, but Aunt Sarum makes—"

"Tut, tut! My dear, you want more than that, you want protecting everywhere, and against everything. Confide in me. I will protect you. Take this bottle and drink its contents. You must drink it all if you want to be thoroughly protected."

"It would be very nice to be protected," said Clara, "for some of those beasts are rather terrifying." She looked up into the fatherly face of the Dodo and could not help having confidence in him; he was so ponderous and bland.

She took the bottle in her hand. "Is it nice?" she asked.

"Delicious, my dear," he replied. "It is all sugar on the top and there are lots of plums in it."

Clara had noticed the Red Queen, standing by the door and eyeing her narrowly, and every now and then when the Dodo

wasn't looking, she seemed to be signing to Clara not to drink
the stuff

Clara hesitated

"Come, come, my dear," said the Dodo, persuasively. "It's so
nice, besides it will make you grow out of all conscience. Drink
it up."

She uncorked the bottle cautiously, and sniffed at the
contents. It was quite white, and didn't smell nasty; besides
Clara had a vague ambition to become something big. The Red
Queen was still beckoning to her, but Clara threw prudence to
the winds and took a sip.

Certainly she was growing—

Crash! Bang!!

What was the matter? Clara had shot up so rapidly that her
head had struck the chandelier, and the shock had caused her
to drop the bottle, which now lay shattered by her far-off feet.

"Ah! You foolish girl," cried the Dodo, angrily, "you have
lost your chance of becoming one of us. Unless the whole is
swallowed the effect will not last. See, you are shrinking again

already. You naughty child," he continued, working himself up into a passion, "you have wasted all that old and crusted spirit of conservatism; and there is very little of the genuine article left in the country. We can only get the real thing in China now, and we have found the Chinese article very expensive lately."

"Oh, please!" sobbed Clara. "I'm so sorry—I'm sure, I—"

"What would have happened I really don't know," said Clara, afterwards, "he was so angry."

Just then, however, the Red Queen saved the situation by rushing furiously up to the Dodo. "Why ca'n't you leave the girl alone?" she cried, and turning to Clara, she said, "The Dodo's aims are too high for you, my dear. What you want is speed, not height. Come along with me."

Seizing Clara unceremoniously by the hand, she hurried her off the terrace. Out into the country they sped at a terrible rate which was ever increasing. It was not running. It was not flying. It was shooting. On, on, they shot till the little girl was giddy and terrified.

"Stop! Stop! I'm a—fraid—I—ca'n't—go—your—pace," gasped Clara.

CHAPTER II

A Mushroom Caterpillar

"Faster! Faster!" cried the Red Queen, as she dragged Clara along until the breath had nearly left her body, and she felt as if cold water were being poured down her back.

"Where are you taking me to?" Clara panted, "I ca'n't help thinking—"

"If you want to do *that*," said the Red Queen, "you and I must part. I never permit any one to think in my presence. It's rude; it's unnecessary."

Saying this, she let go her hand, with the unkind remark that there wasn't room for both of them in the same country.

"When," she continued, icily, "you know more I'll take you up again; then perhaps you will follow me blindfold, and wo'n't get giddy. Meanwhile I leave you here. It is an excellent place for acquiring knowledge, though let me advise you to believe nothing you see, and only half you read, even in print."

With that the Red Queen sped away on her reckless course, leaving Clara in the centre of a vast desolate plain, covered with newspapers, arranged in black and white squares, something like a chestnut board.

Clara knew that no good little girl ever reads such things as newspapers, and, indeed, she prided herself on never having dipped into one in all her life. So you see she did not quite like the place in which she found herself

In the distance, however, she espied an old and withered chestnut-tree to which she determined to make her way, "for," as she very wisely said to herself, "chestnuts are always safe; I remember how pleased they all were when I brought some into the house last Thursday."

Just as she got to the chestnut-tree she noticed a tall mushroom, on the top of which was seated a very green Caterpillar, who was writing at a great pace, and imbibing gas through the tube of a strangely constructed hookah.

Picking up a signed article which had fallen off the mushroom, Clara saw that the insect belonged to the species *Winstoniensis Vulgaris.*

For some hours the Caterpillar took no notice of her, and she was beginning to think that she had better go away without disturbing it, when it slowly raised its head, and, without removing the pipe from its lips, remarked acidly, "YOU'RE WRONG!"

"But," said Clara, "I haven't said anything."

"I know you haven't, and that is wrong, and when you do say something that is wrong too."

"But why am I wronger than other people?"

"I didn't say you were. Everybody is wrong, and I am here to tell them so."

"And how do you think you will put them right?"

"I don't think; I talk. I don't put them right. It takes me all my time to tell them they are wrong. The point is—what do you want?"

"I'm not quite sure, if you please, Sir," said Clara, timidly, "things are so funny today."

"Things are never funny; they are only wrong," said the Caterpillar. "You are not sure what you want; I am. What you want is advice."

"But you ca'n't think what a lot of advice I've had today," replied Clara, distractedly, "and I don't think it's done me one bit of good."

"That's because it wasn't mine," said the Caterpillar. "I shall now read you the leading article I am cabling home."

"I didn't know people ever cabled leaders," said Clara.

"*People* don't, but I do," he replied.

"Is it very long?"

"It is long, but it's very, very clever. It has been written entirely for your improvement."

Clara felt that after this she could not refuse to listen, and the Caterpillar still sucking the pipe, from which it seemed to draw its inspiration, read, as follows:—

Porlokrocky

'Tis warrig and the slinky Pros
Do snibe and squirgle in the dark;
All boersome are the interfoes,
And the frogrags outyark.

Beware the Porlokrock, my Joe!
The Orange Peel, the Olive patch!
Beware the Brussels Spouts, and O!
Mark well the Kaiserspatch.

They packed their Milner to the Cape:
Long time they drawled on this and that—
So footled they on the dum-dum lay,
And piffled as they sat.

And as in snifty mood they piffed,
The Porlokrock, with soul aflame,
Came slimming through the spruity drift,
Pom-pomming as he came!

One!—two!—three!—four! disasters came,
The buckled blades went snipper snap;
They left it dead—That's what they said,
Vermilioning the map.

And will you slay the Porlokrock?
(Come to Pall Mall, my brittle Brod!)
Perchauce you may, if some fine day
You catch him on the nod.

> *'Tis warrig and the slinky Pros*
> *Do snibe and squirgle in the dark;*
> *All boersome are the interfoes,*
> *And the frograps outyark.*

"Thank you, Sir," said Clara, when the Caterpillar had finished. "I'm very much obliged to you, but I ca'n't *quite* understand it."

"I never expected you would," said the Caterpillar.

"But is it any good to give people advice when they don't understand?" asked Clara, in a puzzled tone.

"Of course it is," answered the Caterpillar. "It teaches them how stupid they are."

"I know I'm stupid," said poor Clara, very humbly. "At least everybody seems to think so today, and yet there was a time when they all praised me, and said how clever I was."

"Ah!" remarked the Caterpillar. "That must have been before you tried to keep pace with the Red Queen, wasn't it?"

"Yes," said Clara, almost in tears. "I may be silly, but Aunt Sarum will tell you that I know my lessons by heart, and I can say poetry too—so there!"

"What can you say?"

"Well, do you know," said Clara, brightening up, "when I saw you sitting up there writing so hard I could not help thinking of '*How doth the little busy bee*'?"

"Repeat it," said the Caterpillar, in a somewhat softened tone.

And Clara, putting her hands behind her back, began:—

> *How doth the arm-chair strategist*
> *Improve each censored cable,*
> *Converting it by natty twist,*
> *Into egregious fable.*

> *So airily he seems to write,*
> *So redolent his leader*
> *Of personalities and spite,*
> *It flabbergasts the reader.*

"Oh, dear me!" said Clara, "I'm afraid that wo'n't do. Your leading article put me out. What does *warrig* mean?"

"*Warrig* means the time when you begin to prepare for a war which is nearly over."

"I see," said Clara, "and I suppose *slinky Pros* are sly and slinking Pro-Boers."

"Of course," said the Caterpillar, "and to *snibe* is to sneer and jibe, and to *sguirgle* is to squirm and wriggle, while a *frograg* is a foreign newspaper, and *outyarking* is saying the sort of things foreign newspapers do say. Now try, '*You are old, Father William*'," said the Caterpillar, condescendingly. "Shut your eyes and take a long breath."

So Clara made a fresh start:—

"You are old, Father Johnnie," the Strategist said,
  "And it's years since you'd had a tough fight;
Yet you thought you could shoot that WILDEBEESTE *on your*
    head—
  Do you think, after all, you were right?"

"In my youth," said John Bull, "I developed my hand
  "Upon Arabs, and Niggers, and such;
And I thought that these Boers were of similar brand;
  But I found I was out of it—much."

"You are old, Father John, as I mentioned before,
  And your body and ways are not slim—
Did you think that by bouncing on Stead's 'brother Boer'
  You could knock out the stuffing from him?"

"In my youth," said John Bull, "it was ever my plan
  To win victory after defeat;
And I certainly thought that, the worse I began,
  The better my chances to beat."

"You are old, Father John, and your teeth must be few,
  For your cheeks are both sunken and hollow;
Yet this trashy and most indigestible stew,
  Pray, how do you manage to swallow?"

"In my youth," said John Bull, "I gave appetite scope
  Upon kingdoms and countries galore.
Now with Salisbury's peptonized bluff and soft soap,
  I can swallow just that and no more."

'You are old, Father John, one could hardly have guessed
   That your nerve allows nothing to fright you;
Yet I notice you cherish that snake in your breast—
   Pray, aren't you afraid it will bite you?"

"In my youth," said john Bull, "I always was told
   The vilest of beasts not to hurt;
This one's creepy, and crawly, and clammy and cold,
   But his venom ca'n't get through my shirt."

"Oh, dear me," groaned the Caterpillar, "that's worse than ever. You seem to have strategists on the brain. I think you were better with the 'Busy bee' than with this. Try that over again, and remember that it is about bees, not strategists."
   So Clara tried once more:—

How doth a timely vulture lend
Improvement to a tale,
A Verne-Münchhausen-Crusoe blend,
Which makes de Rougemont pale.

"There, that's quite enough!" screamed the Caterpillar, highly incensed. "Run away and play. Go and bother Crumpty-Bumpty, or Twiddle-Thumb and Twaddle-D."

"But *do* tell me that vulture tale," pleaded Clara, "I should so love to hear it from you. Why did it keep following you from Pretoria? Why are the birds so fond of you? I have read of people who are always seeing snakes, and Aunt Sarum says she could make Frenchmen see stars any time of the day, if she liked, but of course she doesn't, she's *so* kind. Why did that bird follow you?"

"Well, you see," said the Caterpillar, "birds are like human beings; they are wrong. Now that silly bird, in spite of my strikingly handsome appearance—"

He stopped abruptly.

"Well," said Clara, encouragingly, "please don't stop, it's getting so exciting."

"Well then, that bird, you must know, was very hungry, and when it saw me, a brilliant mushroom caterpillar, its idea was to treat me merely as a little grub."

"That was certainly rather humiliating," said Clara, sympathetically, "but after all grubs and caterpillars are rather alike. Why didn't it eat you?"

"It might have done *that*, had it not been for my verbal armour. You see the vulture couldn't swallow my statements."

"And how did you get rid of it?" asked Clara.

"You wo'n't tell anybody if I tell you?" said the Caterpillar.

"No."

"Well, then I sang to it."

"Can you sing?" asked Clara, clasping her hands rapturously together.

"Oh! quite easily; I sang to him:—

> *Swallow on, swallow on;*
> *You may eat whate'er you see,*
> *You may even swallow Official Reports,*
> *But you'll never swallow me.*

"When I gave him 'The Belle of New York', he flew away," said the Caterpillar, turning round to the spot where Clara had been standing.

But Clara, like the vulture, had flown.

CHAPTER III

The Conservatory

"No! They'll never swallow him, that's certain," said Clara to herself as she fled from the plain of dead chestnuts. "What a talkative creature to be sure, and how beautifully green he is! No! They'll never swallow him—but I do wish that vulture had."

After she had run a mile or two through the desert she came across a little house on the door of which was written:—

THE CONSERVATORY.

"This," she said, joyfully, "looks just like home. I'm sure they will be glad to see me if I go in."

A polite old frog-gardener opened the little door for her, and she found herself at once in a small kitchen which was full of fog from one end to the other.

The Duchess was sitting on tenter-hooks nursing a baby which seemed to dislike the process very much. At any rate the poor little thing screamed and howled, without intermission, which was not very surprising, as the Duchess alternately slapped and pinched it, and occasionally put a wet blanket on its head.

The Cook, in the intervals of stirring the soup, hurled everything she could think of at the baby's head, and frequently threw dust in its eyes. "In order," she said, "to arouse it to a sense of its responsibilities."

The Duchess did not seem to mind the pots and pans, even when they hit her, which wasn't often, and she seemed pleased whenever the Dalmeny Cat, who appeared to be trying to escape observation in a hot corner of the kitchen, got a particularly hard knock.

"You see," she said to Clara, "that Cat does not really belong to this house."

"How do you make it stop here?" asked Clara. "Have you buttered its feet?"

"We've buttered it all over, my dear, at times, and yet it wo'n't stop."

"It seems a very nice Cat," said Clara; "but I don't see that it will be much use here, and I'm sure there's no room for it in this pokey little kitchen."

"Ah! my dear, you don't know what respectability a real Dalmeny Cat, one that can appear and disappear just as it likes, and that does nothing but sneer, lends to an establishment of this sort. We found it, 'mee-yowing' in a lonely furrow, sneering so dreadfully because the people next door had turned it out, that we determined to offer it a home.

All this time the Cat dld nothing but sneer at Clara, and wink solemnly, as if it understood all about the Duchess and the baby, and the Cook; and Clara thought to herself it wouldn't stop long in their company.

"Please, would you tell me," said Clara, "why your Cat mews like that?"

"It's because it knows we ca'n't put salt on its tail. You see it hasn't got one now; it lost it when it quarrelled with Crumpty-Bumpty, and now nobody can persuade it to stop more than a week anywhere."

"What a very unsatisfactory Cat," said Clara, "I must say I never expected to see it in this house."

"No, my dear, you wouldn't, and perhaps you didn't expect to find that Cook here either; but if you knew the nasty spiteful things people have been saying about my keeping the whole kitchen for my nephews and nieces, you wouldn't wonder at it. Nobody can say that the Cook, who is really only a charwoman from over the way, or the Cat, are relations of mine."

The baby was getting blacker and blacker in the face, and it was hard to say whether it disliked the Duchess, the Cook, or the Cat, the most. Whenever the Duchess spoke to it, it howled, whenever its eyes fell on the Cook it screamed, and whenever the Cat glanced in its direction it squirmed.

"Here!" said the Duchess to Clara. "You take it and nurse it," and as she spoke she threw it into Clara's arms. "I've got more important things to see to than trying to get an ungrateful little creature like that into a good temper. I've taken a shilling out of its money box already, and I don't believe it would have done it a bit more good if I'd made it eighteen pence, but I'm going to try next year."

Clara caught the baby with some difficulty and carried it outside in the hope of soothing the poor little thing, but its sobs only got more and more like hisses, and its hair more and more like feathers till she became quite excited; "for," as she said to herself "if it is really going to turn into a goose, I think I shall be able to manage it quite nicely."

But everything seemed to go wrong with poor Clara that day, and though the baby looked exactly like a goose in the dim light of the wood into which she had wandered, it turned out to be not half such a goose as it looked when they came out into the daylight.

"Unless you'll promise to be a good obedient little gosling," said Clara, "I wo'n't have anything more to do with you." And as the goose-baby hissed at her again, she let it drop.

"Oh! You cruel girl," it hissed, as it waddled off into obscurity. "I shall go and ask that kind Crumpty-Bumpty to nurse me now."

"There's one comfort," said Clara. "I could never have taken it home, for it might have begun to think for itself, and then what *would* have happened?

"Oh!" cried Clara; for there just above her head, sneering at her from the branches of a gum tree sat the Dalmeny Cat, already escaped from the Duchess's house.

"Up a tree again?" said Clara, when she had got over her shock a little; "I wish you wouldn't always sneer at me like that, you nasty thing. There would be some sense if you would tell me which way I ought to go, but going on sneering and doing nothing else is enough to make one quite cross."

"Smiling, I call it," said the Cat, "not sneering. You should always be polite, even to your superiors."

"Oh, call it what you like," returned Clara, "but *do* stop and tell me where to go."

"Well," said the Cat, "that depends where you want to get to, and you don't seem to know yourself."

"You see," said Clara, "I've tried the Dodo and he's too old-fashioned; and the Red Queen, she's too fast; and the Duchess, she's too slow; and the Caterpillar, he's too—too cock-sure," and she blushed a little at the use of an expression which she knew was slang, for her Aunt had told her never to pay any attention to the words of the man in the street.

"I don't much care where I go," she continued, "so long as I get somewhere."

"You'll do that," said the Cat, "but whether you'll like it or not when you get there I ca'n't say."

"In *that* direction" (waving its right paw) "lives a Hatter; and in *that*" (waving its left) "lives a March Hare. Visit either you like; they're both mad."

"But I don't want to go among mad people."

"Then you shouldn't have come to Blunderland at all. we are all mad here, and if any body isn't mad when he comes, we very soon make him. But it's usually unnecessary."

As it was speaking, the Cat began to flicker and change just like the pictures in a biograph, but, whenever it seemed likely to turn into something interesting, it always faded and went out with a fizzle, leaving nothing behind it but the sneer, which was always there.

"I *do* wish you wouldn't go on chopping and changing like that," Clara cried at last. "You'll really make me Dizzy."

"Oh dear NO!" said the Cat. "You'll never be *that*."

CHAPTER IV

The Mad Party

*A*t a turning of the road Clara came upon the March Hare and the Grey Hatter at tea, and she thought it would be only polite to join their Party; "although," said Clara, "it must only be temporary, of course."

There was a table under a tree, and an essentially Liberal Dormouse was seated at it between the Hatter and the Hare. "Very uncomfortable for the Dormouse," thought Clara; for the Hatter and the March Hare were resting their elbows upon it, and talking over its head. "But then," said Clara to herself, "they always do talk over everybody's head." And saying this, she sat down at the table.

"No room! No room!" cried the March Hare, with a strong Irish brogue.

"There's *plenty* of room!" said Clara. "Why, there are more tea-cups than people, ever so many. Besides, I didn't know it was *your* table."

This made the March Hare laugh a great deal. "It isn't a table at all," he said. "It's a platform. It's not *all* mine. The part above board belongs to him—" pointing to the Hatter with his spoon "—and all the rest to me. The Dormouse thinks he has a share in it too, but he hasn't. That's only our fun, you know."

"Your views want broadening," said the Hatter, suddenly. He had been looking at Clara for some time with great curiosity.

"Why?" asked Clara.

"You'd understand the Dormouse then," answered the Hatter, "and you'd see how splendid it is to sit as we do with it in the middle. I ca'n't abide the March Hare, and the March Hare, he doesn't really like me, but you see, we can each talk to the Dormouse. Our Liberal Party we call it."

"But don't you have differences among yourselves?" asked Clara.

The Dormouse groaned in its sleep.

"Differences! Differences!" cried the Hatter. "Why, that's the whole point of the matter. If we didn't have differences we should go to sleep, like that thing," jogging the Dormouse with his elbow as he spoke.

"Don't you think," asked Clara, "don't you think you would be happier if you did go to sleep?"

"If they only would!" sighed the Dormouse.

"What century is this?" asked the Hatter suddenly, pulling out his watch and banging it on the table.

"It's the beginning of the eighteenth," Clara answered.

"Getting very near Doomsday as far as you're concerned," muttered the Dormouse, looking sleepily at Clara with one eye.

"The hands go round different ways," sighed the Hatter. "I told you dynamite wouldn't suit the works!" he added, looking angrily at the Hare.

"It was the *best* non-explosive," the Hare replied, meekly.

"Yes, but it must have got mixed with some continental gas," the Hatter grumbled. "You shouldn't have put it in by Moonlight."

"The Dormouse is asleep again!" cried the Hare, angrily, and he poured some dreadfully hot water upon its nose.

The Dormouse shook its head impatiently, and said, without opening its eyes, "Of course, of course; just what I was going to remark myself. Hear, hear; hear, hear!"

"Does the Dormouse ever open both its eyes?" asked Clara.

"Only when it gets right into the hot water," said the Hare. "That makes it open its eyes, I can tell you."

"But why does it get into hot water at all?" Clara asked.

"I'm always putting it there," said the Hare.

"You see," said the Hatter, "this Dormouse is such a sleepy old thing, that if I alone were on this side to keep it awake it would go to sleep on the other. So we have to sit on both sides of it, and when we both begin pinching it together you have no idea how it wakes up. Why it even speaks, then!"

"What does it say?" asked Clara.

"O, the first thing that comes into its head," replied the Hatter.

"Generally something foolish!" cried the Hare, thumping the Dormouse in the side.

"Quite so, quite so," sighed the poor Dormouse. "Hear, hear; certainly, certainly."

"Has it a mind of its own?" asked Clara.

"It had once," replied the Hare, "but not since I got hold of its tail. Its mind belongs to me now."

"Half of it," snapped the Hatter.

"All of it," said the Hare

"That's ridiculous," retorted the Hatter. "You may have got the tail, but I've got the whig end, anyhow."

"Were the halves of different sizes?" asked Clara, whose head was beginning to spin.

"Some of them," answered the Hatter.

At this point the Hatter pinched the Dormouse on one side, and the Hare pinched it on the other, and both cried: "Wake up, and say something! Wake up, and say something!"

"Yes, do," said Clara.

"Once upon a time there were three little sisters," the Dormouse began, in a great hurry; "and their names were Patty, Primrose, and Plantagenetta; and they lived at the bottom of a well—"

"Why?" asked Clara.

"Because they thought Truth was there," answered the Dormouse.

"And was it?" Clara asked.

"Only a weekly edition," sighed the Dormouse.

"And what did they live on?" asked Clara.

"Mostly on things beginning with an M," replied the Dormouse "such as mistakes, mysteries, muddles, mortification, and mudlarks."

"They couldn't have done that, you know," Clara gently remarked. "They'd have been ill."

"So they were," said the Dormouse. "*Very* ill."

"What happened?" Clara asked.

"They quarrelled," sighed the Dormouse. "Primrose said they must have a big house, Plantagenetta said a little one would do, and Patty said she must have one of her own with a large nursery for her grievances."

"And did they part?" Clara asked.

"Nobody knows, they don't even know themselves."

"How foolish of them," said Clara. "But what did they do?"

"O, they went on quarrelling," said the Dormouse.

"Was that all?" asked Clara.

"It took up all their time," explained the Dormouse.

"And are they still at the bottom of the well?" said Clara.

"No; they're at the bottom of the poll now," sighed the Dormouse; "and it's very uncomfortable."

"After that—" said the Hare to the Hatter, in a threatening tone.

"I quite agree," said the Hatter. "The Dormouse must be suppressed."

All this time Clara had been getting very hungry, and at last she said, "Aren't you going to get on with your tea? I think I should like to have an egg, please."

"You ca'n't have one now," said the Hatter. "They're not in season, you must wait for the elections. But you shall have some potted Dormouse, if you wait."

Thereupon the March Hare and the Hatter seized the wretched Dormouse and forced it into the teapot.

"And now, my dear," said the Hare, "if you will hold out your cup—"

This was more than Clara could stand, so she jumped up and ran away.

CHAPTER V

Crumpty-Bumpty

*P*erhaps it was because Clara was thinking so much about the egg, which she did not get at the Mad Party, that the appearance of something round and white in the distance caught her eye almost at once as she walked away. When she came nearer the thing got more and more like a real egg until, as she came close up to it, she exclaimed, in surprise, "Why, it's Crumpty-Bumpty himself, and how exactly like an egg he is!" It was indeed that celebrated character, and, just as she expected, he was sitting on a wall.

For some time Clara gazed at him in silence, admiring the immense expanse of cheek he presented to the public, and the skill with which he maintained his position on the wall.

Meanwhile Crumpty-Bumpty gave no sign of life whatever, and Clara began to think he wasn't really alive after all, but only a figure, such as she had often seen at Madame Tussaud's, "in which case," she said, "even a pin-prick will let all the sawdust out."

Unfortunately, she made the last remark out loud, and it seemed to hurt Crumpty-Bumpty's feelings very much indeed,

for his mouth was suddenly opened, and he said, in a very loud and emphatic tone of voice, "I regard you as a barbarian with loathsome methods."

"I beg your pardon, Sir?" said Clara.

"But," he went on, always avoiding Clara's eye, and looking straight in front of him, "when I say 'barbarian', of course I mean a civilized barbarian, and I shall be really displeased if you persist in considering the expression 'loathsome methods' at all censorious. There are many loathsome methods, particularly in war, which are quite nice when you get to know them well, and which ought to be employed on proper occasions. Take special notice, my dear, that I said 'employed', not 'used'. They should never be used."

"It sounds very beautiful, Sir," said Clara, respectfully, "but I'm afraid I don't understand you."

"No?" returned Crumpty-Bumpty. "Well, you mustn't be discouraged. I know it's hard. Why, very often I ca'n't understand what I say myself until it's explained the next morning in the newspapers. There are hundreds of that make a living out of explaining ME. That's what you call fame, you know."

"I don't think I do," said Clara, doubtfully.

"Of course it is," answered Crumpty-Bumpty, impatiently. "Anybody knows that. Don't stand there looking as if you didn't understand, but tell me your name and your business."

"My name's Clara, Miss Clara, and I'm beginning to think that I haven't got any business in Blunderland at all, but—"

"There, there, child, that'll do," interrupted Crumpty-Bumpty. "Of course I could see at a glance that you hadn't; but your name's very pretty and appropriate. It's so expressive."

"Is it?" said Clara, in rather a melancholy tone. "I suppose it is," and tears came into the poor child's eyes.

"Don't cry," said Crumpty-Bumpty, kindly. "Remember it might have been much worse. You might have been christened 'Buckshot'. And now just tell me what it is you want to know, because I suppose you didn't come to see an important person like myself out of curiosity?"

"Oh no, Sir," answered Clara, eagerly, "of course not, nobody would do that. What I really want to know is—whether you would like our soldiers to win in South Africa or not."

"That's a very easy question to answer," said he. "Of course I want them to win, provided, mind you, I say provided, they don't beat the enemy. I could never countenance THAT."

"Couldn't you really?" said Clara, with great curiosity. "It's so interesting to know you want the English to win without the Boers being beaten—or is it the other way about? I never saw anybody at all like you before."

"No, and you wo'n't either," went on Crumpty-Bumpty; "but then you don't know what a wonderful person I am. Why, I can not only sit on a fence for days and days together without ever falling off, but I can sit on both sides of the fence at the same time. There's dexterity for you. That's what you call being a real leader of men."

Clara didn't know what to answer to this, so by way of changing the conversation, she suddenly remarked, "What a beautiful hyphen you've got! At least," she corrected herself "a beautiful equator, I should have said—No, a hyphen, I mean—I beg your pardon," she added in dismay, for Crumpty-Bumpty looked dreadfully offended.

At last he said, angrily, "It's a most provoking thing when a person doesn't know a hyphen from an equator. It's a hyphen, as you ought to know by this time, and it's the most valuable thing in the world. Pulls me together, you know. But it costs a dreadful lot to keep up. It was a present to me from my colleagues, they said I was so changeable that I must wear something by which they could always know me."

"What are colleagues?" asked Clara. "I should like to know so much."

"My dear," said Crumpty-Bumpty, "colleagues are things that fly off at tangents. I've got lots of 'em, and I never know what they'll be up to next; but I've managed to tame a brace of 'em, a Walrus and a Carpenter, both very ferocious specimens. I've taught them to do nearly everything I tell them now. It was all done by kindness, and just as you came along I was composing a poem about them."

"Oh! do say it," cried Clara.

So, hitching up his hyphen, Crumpty-Bumpty began:—

> *The sun was bumping round the sky,*
> *Bumping with all his might,*
> *He did his level best to set*
> *On Britain's Appetite,*
> *But, tho' he always rose betimes,*
> *He couldn't do it quite.*

The moon was chuckling icily,
  Because she said the sun
Was like a little Englander
  (That made him swear like fun),
She said he ought to take a tour
  With Cook or Doctor Lunn.

The ocean serged with navy blue,
  The lands were red as red,
And even clothed in khaki was
  The Tauchnitz which you read,
Ubiquitous Britannia kept
  Apollo out of bed.

The Walrus and the Carpenter
  Were ploughing in the sand,
They wept like one o'clock to see
  Such lots of British land,
"If this belonged to France or Spain,"
  They said, "it would be grand."

"If dear Lloyd George and Honest Burns
In Downing Street did sup,
Do you suppose," the Walrus asked,
"That they could bust us up?"
"Let's try 'em," sighed the Carpenter,
And hic'd dyspeptic cup.

"O Voters, come and join with us,"
The Walrus did beseech,
"As many rads, as many fads,
As little hands can reach;
Bring all the blessed lot, dear friends,
We'll find a hand for each."

The sober Voters looked at him,
Their followers were many,
The sober Voters winked their eye,
And did not give a penny,
Meaning to say, tho' much obliged,
They were not taking any.

But some young Voters hurried up,
All glad to air their views,
They said the Truth was what they sought
(TEREWTII's the word they use).
And this is odd, because, you see,
They read the D——ly N—ws!

The Walrus and the Carpenter
Talked on, but no more came,
And so they sat them down to think,
And said it was a shame,
While all the foolish Voters said—
"Now, what's your little game?"

"The time has come," the Walrus said,
"To talk like Mother Gamps,
Of pubs, and pumps, and Chamberlain,
Of Concentration Camps,
And how our military men
Are murderers and scamps."

"But half a mo'!" the Voters said,
"This talk may go too far,
For some of us have friends, and some
Have children at the War."
The Carpenter, he cleared his throat,
"We blame the offisAR!"

"The Upper Class," the Walrus said,
"Is what we must attack,
The Private is a moral man,
We knife the General's back,
Now if you're ready, Voters dear,
We can begin to hack."

"But how is this?" the Voters cried,
Turning a little white,
"This wo'n't increase a daily wage
And help a bloke get tight!"
"The end is pure," the Walrus said,
"Did you admire John Bright?"

"Yours is the power to turn the scale,
Yours is the hand we lick."
The Carpenter said nothing but,
"Give Joe another brick.
I wish you wouldn't wander so,
It's him we've got to stick."

"It seems a shame," the Walrus said,
  "To let our programme go,
Might we not give Home Rule a turn,
  Or bring the High Church low?"
The Carpenter said nothing but,
  "Dash it, get on to Joe!"

"I weep for him," the Walrus said,
  "All strife I deprecate,"
With studious care he sorted out
  Words of infernal hate,
Hurling with might at Joseph's head
  The fishiest Billingsgate.

"O Voters!" cried the Carpenter,
  "When all is said and done,
Shall we not turn the Tories out?"—
  But answers came there none,
And this was scarcely odd; they had
  Disgusted everyone!

"They're nasty, horrid, things, but I don't hate the Walrus as much as the Carpenter, he wasn't quite so spiteful," said Clara.

"No! But he was more blood-thirsty," said Crumpty-Bumpty.

"Then I like the Carpenter best."

"Ah! But he was as blood-thirsty as he dare be."

"Well, then I hate them both," said Clara. "Tell me something about the others. I'm sure you must have some nice colleagues somewhere."

"No end of them," said Crumpty-Bumpty. "All the colours of the rainbow. But you'd better go and see them. I keep all my bright specimens in my garden. It's a beautiful spot, and it's called Boerdom."

"But it's too hot for gardens," pleaded Clara.

"But Boerdom is a very shady place, I can tell you," said Crumpty-Bumpty, and he pointed away to the Extreme Left.

The effort nearly caused him to overbalance himself.

"Oh! Do take care, you're so roly-poly, you know," cried Clara, and she went on anxiously, "I'm sure you must get giddy up there."

"Everybody says I'm giddy," said Crumpty-Bumpty, "but I'm not, though I admit I feel a bit addled at times. But it's better for me to maintain my equilibrium, for," he continued, with great solemnity, "I'm always afraid that if I were to fall, I should become quite cracked."

"That *would* be dreadful," said Clara, "besides I think I've read somewhere that, *All the King's horses, and all the King's men, couldn't—*"

"Of course they couldn't. They'd have a try though. But they couldn't do it without money. Money will do anything. But you see I'm not a Jingo, so I ca'n't say, 'I've got the money too.' I went to see the man with the money the other day, and tried to persuade him to promise to have me mended, but he was very deaf. At last I bawled in his ear, 'If I were to fall what *would* happen?'"

"Did he hear that?" asked Clara. "What did he say?"

"He only said, 'I should smile.'"

"How horrid of him," said Clara, indignantly. "What would become of you, then?"

"Well," said Crumpty-Bumpty, with a wink, "I have a card up my sleeve. The other day I held a secret meeting to which the newspapers were invited—some of them—and I made them promise that, whenever I fall, they will patch me up somehow."

"And can they do it, do you think?" asked Clara.

"Of course they can. Newspaper people are so handy with paste and scissors."

"It would be very difficult," said Clara. "Come! You had better let me help you off the wall. I'm a very careful little girl, and I'm sure I should let you down more gently than some people I know."

"Would you really, my dear?" said Crumpty-Bumpty, and he put out his hand. But poor little Clara was not quite tall enough, and in the effort to touch her fingers Crumpty-Bumpty overbalanced, and fell with a

CRASH!!!!

to the ground.

Clara hid her face, and began to cry a little. When she opened her eyes again, she saw, standing among a lot of broken egg-shell, two fat little men. They were so exactly alike that no one could have told them apart except for the names on their collars.

"Ah!" they exclaimed together. "You didn't expect that, did you? That's what you call a political metamorphosis, that is."

"Why, I do declare," cried Clara, "you're two dear little Crumpty-Bumpties," for I she saw the hyphen was still there, though it now seemed to link the two men. "How in the world did you change like that?"

"We *were* Crumpty-Bumpty, but we are not now. We disown him," they said, together.

"I'm Twiddle-Thumb," said one.

"I'm Twaddle-D, with a very big D," said the other.

"I'm purely ornamental," said Twiddle-Thumb.

"I'm perfectly useless," said Twaddle-D.

Clara was rather confused, and did not quite know what to do. She was anxious, as always, to make herself pleasant. At last she said, "I should think you were more comfortable when you were one person. It must be dreadfully confusing to come in two like that."

"Nohow!" cried Twiddle-Thumb.

"Contrariwise!" said Twaddle-D. "You see when we had the misfortune to be one person we were always fighting inside Crumpty-Bumpty, and that upset his digestion most dreadfully. In fact it was our pulling different ways that really brought him down."

"You've no idea of the difficulties it got us into," said Twiddle-Thumb.

"Why, there was that unfortunate message to the Tail, and all that. Did you never hear of it?" said Twaddle-D. And without waiting for Clara to reply, the two little men began to repeat together, and in exactly the same tone, this poem:—

> *I sent a message to the Tail,*
> *I asked them, "Is the show to fail?"*
>
> *The party Tail they did agree*
> *To send an answer back to me.*

The Tail replied with much regret,
"We will support you, Sir, and yet—"

I sent to them again to say,
"It must be either Aye or Nay!"

The Tail made answer, with a pooh!
"This isn't, Sir, a bit like you."

I held a meeting large and strong,
I made a speech, and it was long.

I said "I'll end this Dreadful Mess,
I'll abdicate at once, unless—"

Then some one came to me and said,
"The Tail has really lost its head."

I said to him, I said it plain,
"The Tail has everything to gain."

But he was very old and chill,
He said he worshipped me, but still—

I took a corkscrew from the Shelf,
I boldly tried to draw myself.

And when I saw that I was double,
I said it saved a deal of trouble,

And when I found the door unshut,
I swore that I was happy, but—

"Is that all?"asked Clara, surprised at the sudden stoppage of the voices in the middle of a sentence.

"Yes," they answered together. "You can invent the rest for yourself. You see we have to please so many people that we always talk like missing-word competitions. They're very popular, and anybody can guess what they like."

Clara was getting tired of the twins. "Please," she said, "can you tell me where Crumpty-Bumpty's beautiful garden is situated?"

"It isn't *situated*" said Twaddle-D. "It *lies*—over there."

"Is there no one to show me the way?"said Clara.

B o e r d o m

"Nohow, my dear," said Twiddle-Thumb. "I cannot go with you."

"Contrariwise," said Twaddle-D, "you must go by yourself."

Then they said together, "You see, we cannot both go the same way, and we cannot separate from each other. The Hyphen would be angry," and with that they left her.

"Perhaps it's as well," thought Clara, "for they don't seem able to walk straight. Probably they're inebriated with the exuberance of their own verbosity."

She was not sorry, then, to get rid of the twins; they were too talkative for her. Besides she was not *quite* sure she agreed with *all* they said. You see they talked in such a contradictory way.

She was, however, delighted to go into the garden all by herself, for she was a dreamy child, and loved flowers, "and, when you are by yourself, you know," she said, "there's nobody to tell you to keep off the grass, and all that sort of thing."

There didn't seem to be any fence or wall round the place, but there was a sort of line which indicated in a vague way the limits of the garden. When she came nearer she saw that what had looked like a line was really a deepish ditch, at which a number of ordinary-looking people seemed to be digging.

"What are you all doing that for?" asked Clara, of a man in the street.

"Well, I'm not very particular, miss, but I'm drawing the line here," he answered. "We all are, and I advise you to do so, too. It's a nasty place you're going into there."

"Oh! What a story-teller Crumpty-Bumpty must be," thought Clara. "He said that everything in the garden was lovely. Why!" she continued, turning to the man. "They told me, for one thing, that it was full of beautiful creepers."

"So it is," he answered. "There are plenty of creepers, and crawlers as well. They are beauties too, the lot of 'em; but that's not my idea of a garden."

"But you see I'm not going to stay," said Clara, disheartened; "I'm only going to see what it's like." And she wandered dreamily on.

At last she came to an archway over which was written the word *Boerdom*, and, with a little shiver, she walked through. "This *is* a dirty place," she said, as she passed under the archway. "It's more like a menagerie than a garden."

She found herself standing close by a thing like a water butt, and all round her were hideous creatures, "just like," as she explained, "the things that come and sit on your chest in bed after you've been dining with the Souls."

"These must be the creepers," said she.

But Clara was a brave little girl, and she went straight up to one of the beasts, who had a screw nose, and who was trying to bore holes in a fat Gilded Mug lying on the ground.

"What *are* you doing? I'm sure you will break it if you aren't careful," said Clara.

"That's all right!" growled the odd beast. "It's only my play; I'm not really a-tryin' to smash the old Mug, not me! Why, I couldn't get on without it.

"I wasn't thinking of the Mug. It was your poor nose," answered Clara. "Isn't it very sore?"

"Oh, it burns a bit," said the creature. "But it's been put out of joint long ago by these other animals. I'm only here, you know, because just now there ain't nothink in my line to do elsewhere. That's to say nothing striking. You see I'm one of the 'orny 'anded myself—one of them blokes wot's willin' to work, but wo'n't. I've always got to seem to be a-pickin' 'oles in somethin' or else my mates wouldn't keep me goin'."

"What are you?" asked Clara.

"By purfession," said the beast, "I'm wot they call a 'anger-on."

"I've never heard of that as a plant, but it sounds like a sort. of creeper," mused Clara. "And what are those things that look like hedgehogs walking about on hairpins?"

"Those are the Slinky Pros you heard about before. They're called Pros, you see, because they're against everything English."

"Then they ought to be called Antis not Pros."

"So they did, miss, but you see they're for everything that's anti-English, and there are such a lot of respectable Antis that we were obliged to call 'em Pros."

"And are those other things pigs?"

"Lor bless yer, miss, those ain't pigs. They're Welsh rabbits, leastwise two on 'em is, and the third one with his back to you, 'e's no class, so we just lumps 'im in with them. Them two real Welsh rabbits is very fine specimens. One is the amateur Bobby of Llanystumdwy, and the other is known as the chess-playing Bunny of Llandymwunblwothbellllt."

"And what are they doing here?" asked Clara.

"Ca'n't you see? They're snorting in the air."

"What good does that do?"

"It annoys the neighbours."

"And why do you all keep on waltzing round this old water butt?"

"It ain't a water butt. It's a tub for thumping. You see we must thump something, and that ca'n't hit us back."

"Are there no flowers in this garden?" said Clara. "I mean, of course," she added, politely, "except the creepers."

"Why, we're all flowers here. We're daisies, I can tell you."

"That old Pro there, with the spectacles," said Clara, "I'm sure he isn't a flower."

"Of course 'e is, miss; why, 'e's the flower of the flock."

"No, but I mean real flowers, on stalks, you know."

"Oh yes! You'll find more than you want if you go along that path and turn round the corner."

So Clara went on and soon came to a flower bed with the strangest flowers she had ever seen in her life. Instead of box, or grass, or tiles, the beds were edged with dead cats, half bricks, and very inexpensive eggs, and the flowers themselves had faces with flat noses and thick lips.

Though Clara never read newspapers, her Aunt allowed her sometimes, when she had been good, to look at the pictures in the weekly ones, and so she knew who these flower-people were. There were Dr Leyds, and Mr Hoffmeyer, and Mr Steyn, and Herr von Schreiner, and ever so many more.

"It's no use my talking to *them*," she said. "They can only speak double Dutch, and I shouldn't believe what they said if I did understand it." So she walked along, with her head in the air.

What a lot there were, to be sure!

Cronje, and Smuts, and Te Water, and Delarey, and Viljoen, and Grobelaar, and—and—Yes! There he was, and she clapped her hands for joy.

Yes!

It was de Wet.

"Now I have got you," she cried, and tried to pick him. "For," said she, "Auntie would so like to put him in water."

But when she put out her hand she pricked her finger with a thorn. "Oh you nasty thing!" she exclaimed, as she sucked the injured linger.

And when she looked up the flower had faded away.

She liked the flowers better than the beasts, however. They were not beautiful, but, at any rate, they looked less creepy than the creeping things.

There were beds and beds of these Boer flowers, but she missed one face, and a face Clara knew far better than all the others. "Why isn't it here?" she asked herself, and just then she saw three gardeners busily painting a large rose tree. s

"That's a funny thing for gardeners to be doing," she said to herself, as she went up to them.

"How dare you?" she said angrily, for she had heard that it was the height of folly to try and paint the lily, and knew it must be quite as bad to colour the rose.

"Hush, my dear!" said one of the gardeners, who had just finished wrangling with the others. "Don't make a noise. You see, we're a-paintin' of old Kroojer's face on all these flowers, because he's left this garden long ago. He's made his pile and gone into private life, and he don't take no interest in the place now. But we've got to pretend he's here or else our job would be gone. The whole garden would collapse if people knew he was out of it."

And then strange to say it *did* collapse. "Well, not exactly collapse," explained Clara, to Geraldine, when she was telling her of these wonderful adventures. "The flowers and the gardeners seemed to be lost in obscurity, and I found myself close to a very thick wood."

CHAPTER VII

Beknighted

On the edge of the wood Clara suddenly came across a most curious figure riding towards her on something that looked partly like a horse, but more like an obstinate old Bull.

The rider was dressed in white armour of very old pattern, and she wondered whether he really went into battle in such antiquated harness, and could not help thinking that it was a wonder that he came out alive, if he did. On his head was a helmet shaped like a donkey's head so that she could not see his face. She was sorry for this, as she was sure that he must be a funny-looking man.

His horse was hung around with strange weapons—a broken wooden sword which did not look as if it could ever have done much damage even when new, and a heavy spiked club with which he belaboured his old horse, whose hide, however, was fortunately very thick.

Just as Clara was about to run away and hide herself from this terrifying creature, she heard a voice in the distance, shouting, "Ulti-ulti-ulti-matum!" and a Knight in red armour dashed out of the wood on the other side.

Coming up to the other, he saluted gravely, and said, "We will have a Peace Conference, and then a fight."

The White Knight, after thinking for some time, remarked, "You will, I presume, observe the Rules of Battle."

"Certainly," replied the other. "You will observe *your* rules, and I'll observe *mine*."

"That is fair," said the White Knight. "I will now read you my rules so that there shall be no mistake."

Thereupon he took from his pocket a lengthy paper, and after clearing his throat, began:—

"RULE 1. *Whereas* I bind myself to bind myself with every sort of restriction.

"RULE 2. *Whereas* the aforesaid ME engages himself that I shall only use the oldest weapons obtainable, unless there are others still older.

"RULE 3. *Whereas it being understood* that I of the one part am not to fire on red crosses on white flags.

"RULE 4. *Moreover*, any prisoners taken in fair fight by the hereinbefore ME shall be supplied with feather beds, punkas and electric light, and shall be treated as British Generals.

"RULE 5. *In so much as* I of the one part am to indulge in no Dum Dums or Flank Attacks.

"Do you agree to these terms?"asked the White Knight.

"Yes," said the other. "I understand that you are of the one part, and I am certainly of the other. In other words, as my rules are just the reverse of yours, I need not put you to the trouble of hearing them."

"No," said the White Knight, "I am acquainted with your methods, and I know you will adhere to them strictly, therefore we will proceed to light, each according to his own rules."

Then they went at it hammer and tongs, the Red Knight of course using the hammer, and the White Knight, the tongs.

An unwritten rule seemed to be that each combatant should exclaim at intervals that he had "surrounded" his opponent, whereupon he stood still until the surrounded one knocked him off his horse. After each had been knocked off fourteen times, the battle ended by the Red Knight dismounting his opponent, capturing his tongs, and riding away with them.

For some time the poor White Knight lay unconscious, though Clara did everything she could to bring him to, even burning under his nose a copy of the Report on Army Reform, which she fortunately had in her pocket. The smell of the dead ashes seemed to revive him a little, and when he came to himself, he said to her, with a faint smile, "Thank you, my dear, it was a glorious victory, wasn't it?"

"Well," replied Clara rather doubtfully, "I don't know so much about that. It seemed to me that you got the most hurt, and then he went away with your arms."

"You will see, my dear, that in the censored cable that will be described as 'the enemy having, when things were at their hottest, beaten a hasty and undignified retreat'. I'm afraid," continued the Knight, "you don't understand these things. One of my rules, which I forgot to read out just now, is that, whatever the result may be, the victory always remains on my side. Besides, you know, that fellow had a horse. Think of that!"

"But you've got a horse too," said Clara, "haven't you?"

"Oh yes! of course," replied the Knight, "but then you see I always take it for granted that *nobody* will be fitted out like me."

"Oh! He was much better off for all those things than you," said Clara, hoping to propitiate him.

"I didn't say that he was not *better* equipped than I, but not *like* me. You see, I spend half my time in inventing things for fighting with, and the other half in preventing other people from doing so."

"I don't see how you can keep other people from inventing things," said Clara. "Surely you ca'n't?"

"*You* couldn't," returned the Knight, "but *I* do. You see, I am the great war inventor in these parts. Years and years before you were born I invented a way of saving money by not paying the soldiers their wages. The patent for that, however, has run out long ago, and lots of my opponents follow that plan now. It is the regular practice in countries as far off as China and Turkey."

"But yet," said Clara, "I don't understand how you keep other people from inventing things."

"Well," said the Knight, a beautiful look of peace and contentment suffusing his masked face, "it's done in this way. Everybody has to send his invention to me, and then I put it away in a box, and tell him that I'll let him know about it IN DUE COURSE. I suppose you don't know what 'due course' means, do you?"

"No, I don't," said Clara.

"Ah! You've never had a departmental training, you see. 'Due course' means just when I choose, and I generally don't choose. When I *do* choose, I tell him that his invention isn't any use at all, and that he musn't come bothering us any more. Then he goes away quite satisfied."

"But doesn't he sometimes take it elsewhere?" asked Clara, who was very much puzzled.

The poor Knight looked annoyed. "You ought not to say things like that," he said, very slowly. "They wound my feelings. There have been one or two people who have done that sort of thing, and the worst of it is that that Red fellow, who was here just now, has bought some of their rubbish, which isn't fair."

Clara didn't quite know what to say in answer to this, for the Knight groaned in such a dreadful way when he thought about it that she was quite distressed. so, by way of turning the conversation, she said: "That's a very fine animal you're riding."

"Ah! You may well say that," said the Knight, evidently pleased. "Isn't he? This horse has been in my family for years and years and years, and indeed, he was bred specially for me to ride on."

As he spoke, he pulled the wrong rein, and the horse immediately plunged him into the ditch at the side of the road.

When she had helped the Knight up into the saddle again, Clara said: "If you've had him all that time, I wonder you ca'n't ride better by now."

"The great art of riding," said the Knight, in some surprise, "is to hold your horse in tight on the curb, with a strong red tape bridle. Mine is of the strongest, and if this horse were to kick his hind legs off—and he does kick like a grasshopper sometimes—he couldn't get rid of that, and as long as I hold on tight to the bridle, I am all right. See how easily I guide him."

"You don't guide him at all," thought Clara, to herself, "and I shouldn't be surprised if he were to run away from you altogether some day." But she only said: "Dear me."

Clara was evidently bursting to ask something, but yet she hesitated. At last she said: "And how do you guide yourself? You seem to have rules for everything. What are your rules for your daily life?"

"I invented maxims," said the White Knight, complacently.

"And Nordenfeldts?" suggested Clara, for she was anxious to show off her knowledge.

"No, nothing so paltry as that, a book of maxims, I mean. Here it is. Let me read some of them to you:—

> *Procrastination is the life of the Army,*
> *Spare the Brod and spoil the rates,*
> *Never attack sideways; it isn't fair,*
> *All we fritter is not gold,*
> *Powder should be seen and not felt,*

The Yeoman's pay is far away,
It's a wrong statesman that does no turning,
All work and no pay makes Jack a handy man.

Do you want to hear any more?"

"No, thank you," said Clara. "They are all very nice, I am sure, but do you think these maxims of yours would be sufficient to guide you in an emergency? Supposing you were to have a real war, what then?"

"Don't talk like that, child," the Knight exclaimed, excitedly, "You make my blood run cold. There couldn't be such a thing, but even if there were—mind you, I say if there were—I should be equal to the occasion. Yes! I have made arrangements to deal even with the impossible. What do you think of that?"

"Well! *What* would you do?" asked Clara, breathless with excitement.

"I SHOULD RESIGN," said the Knight, with solemn dignity.

Clara was disappointed. "I knew a man who did that once," she said, "and do you know, the funny thing was that when it was all over they wouldn't have him back. Said they didn't know what they paid him for, and lots of other rude things."

"That's all very well for common people," the Knight rejoined, airily; "but it couldn't happen to me. You see I am what they call an integral factor in the Constitution—you'd better look that out in the dictionary, when you get home— and they *ca'n't* do without me. I'm the only one who can damp military ardour, and I was never so unhappy as when I found I couldn't damp colonial patriotism. Why! I nearly succeeded in keeping the Volunteers in their right place. But for me, the Volunteers would have guns—real guns, mind you; guns that kill people. They are so insanely zealous. Then the colonial troops wanted to be treated like real soldiers. They went to war with the unchristian intention of fighting—and killing. Fighting—pshaw! a brutal thing I've always despised. The colonial troops," he continued, with a groan, "know how to ride, and are prepared to rough it most abominably. Ah! There's nobody else who can snub them into propriety. They say that Nero was a brave man for playing the fiddle while Rome was burning; but bless you, bless you, I should be found fiddling with new caps and things while London was being invaded. That is what the French call *sang froid*, my dear."

And the old Knight, who had been growing more and more excited as his discourse continued, pitched himself off his horse into the ditch again, and snorted.

"Leave me here a while, my dear," he said, to Clara. "My thoughts are more coherently expressed up-side-down."

And the patient old horse winked the other eye at Clara.

Presently the Knight calmed down, and when Clara had packed him into the saddle once more, she said to him, "Tell me something more about your wonderful inventions."

"I will sing to you of the worries of an inventor's life," said he, and he began to the tune of "*I take thy all, I can no more*":—

"*I'll tell thee everything I can,*
    There's plenty to relate,"
Thus spake a weary soldier man,
    A-sitting on a gate.
"*Who are you, weary man?*" *I said,*
    "*How came you to this state?*"
And his answer rattled on my head,
    Like peas upon a plate.

He said, "*Though sitting on this gate*
    May all be very well,
I'm forced to hang about and wait
    Instructions from Pall Mall.
I'm told to stop, and then to go,
    And fight, and stand the racket,
And then, WHATEVER *I may do,*
    The Government don't back it."

But I was thinking of a scheme
    For patching soldiers' boots
With paper, at a bob a ream,
    Made up from cast-off suits.
So, having pigeon-holes to fill
    With "VERY URGENT" *letters,*
I treated all his talk as nil,
    Or insult to his betters.

He said, "*No doubt they'll tell me soon*
    To scramble up a spire,
And fetch for them some buttered moon,
    And set the Thames on fire.
But, fettered in a red tape trap,
    I'm hampered at my movements;
And, though I've got a German cap,
    I've nought in true improvements."

But I was thinking how I could
  Improve our war equipment,
By making swords of tin and wood
  And thus reduce the shipment.
I shook him well from side to side,
  Until I bust his buttons;
"Come tell me what you want," I cried,
  "REVENONS À NOS muttons."

"You say," said he, "I'm lacking care"
  (I hadn't really said it);
"My long report would make you stare,
  But then you've never read it:
À propos! Why make US embark
  On all this futile writing?
You want a continental clerk,
  And not a man for fighting."

"But kindly tell me why you ask
  So many senseless riddles?
Perchance you seek a means to mask
  Your public tarradiddles?
Yours to work out the task has been
  The soldiers' evolution,
I am the outcome of routine—
  Rot and circumlocution."

I heard him then, for I had planned,
  A scheme, by means of plaster
To hide our faces in the sand,
  And thus escape disaster.
I thanked him (I applaud his nerve),
  And made a note by stealth,
That candid officers deserve
  Promotion to the shelf.

And now whene'er I draw my screw,
*   For playing loose and fast,*
I snigger at my sleeve anew,
*   I think upon the past.*
And when my conscience whispers, "O!
*   You've such a dirty slate,"*
I smile, for it reminds me so
Of that poor man I used to know,
Whose ways were blunt, whose methods slow,
Who was with ardour all aglow,
Whose arm could deal sledge-hammer blow,
Who never feared a mortal foe,
Who ran at gate like buffalo,
Who fell like ninepins in a row,
Who counselled "Yes" when we said "No",
Whom we kept dodging to and fro,
Until he knew not where to go,
But never let his gee-gee Whoa!
Who always looked so comme-il-faut,
Who look to war his piano,
And whom we used uncommon low,
I proudly slap my chest and crow;
FOR IT WAS I WHO MADE HIM SO—
*   A-sitting on a gate.*

When he had finished, Clara threw herself down on the grass, and burst into a flood of tears.

"You don't seem to laugh as heartily as I had expected," said the Knight, with a somewhat offended air. "That was a comic song."

"I know, I know," sobbed Clara. "But it seems to me that it was very sad too in places, though perhaps you did not mean it to be so."

With an effort, however, the brave little girl mastered her grief, and started at once on a topic that evidently lay very near heart.

"So you invented the typical soldier, did you?" asked Clara, admiringly. "It was very clever of you. And all those other wonderful inventions of yours, however do you manage it? That last one in your song, you know, about escaping disaster by hiding your face in the sand. That is very wonderful and original."

"Yes, it is very wonderful, and very original," agreed the Knight. "I invented it last week, but would you believe it?" and his helmet bristled as he spoke. "That unscrupulous Foreign Office of ours has been making use of it for years and years and years. I am thinking of prosecuting them for infringement."

"Why don't you point out to them that you invented it, and ask them to give you lots and lots of money for it? I'm sure they would, if they only knew," suggested Clara, who was a very practical little girl.

"Let us try," she continued, for she was very pleased with her idea; and between them they concocted a report on the invention, which Clara wrote in her best copy-book hand on large official paper, of which the White Knight had a plentiful supply.

"How shall we address it?" asked Clara. "Who attends to this sort of communication?"

"That has always been a mystery," said the White Knight. "Address it in a vague way, but be sure and put a very long reference number on the top. Anyone there will understand it. You see they all speak French so nicely at the Foreign Office."

Clara's face had quite brightened up by this time, and she felt that she was on such friendly terms with the old Knight that she could now venture to ask him a question that had been on the tip of her tongue ever since she saw him. So, while she was folding up the letter, she looked up at him, and said, "Oh, *do* tell me why you wear that funny looking thing on your head."

"You see," answered the Knight, evidently pleased, "it is an invention of my own for saving my face in China."

CHAPTER VIII

Friend or F.O.?

"There! *That's* done!" said Clara, as she stuck up the envelope, and gave it a little thump with her fist. "And now who shall we get to take it?"

"You had better go yourself," said the White Knight. "No one would suspect anyone with a face like yours of having an ulterior motive."

"I'd rather not," cried Clara, "I should be afraid. Why don't you go?"

"Tut, tut, child, that shows how little you know of procedure. Why," continued he, with great solemnity, "for one Department to communicate with another in that off-hand manner would constitute a breach of etiquette; it would *create a precedent.*"

"How *awful,*" said Clara, stopping her ears. "Well," said she, more to pacify him than anything else, "there's the Red Queen, she would make a capital messenger; see how fast she runs."

"Excuse me, my dear, this requires serious thought. Allow me to think."

Thereupon the White Knight once more threw himself head foremost into the ditch. His attitude had the desired effect, and at the end of a moment or two his voice was heard. The words sounded, thought Clara, like a phonograph; doubtless because his mouth was half full of dead leaves. "There's no help for it, you must take it yourself."

So Clara, like the obedient little girl she was, started off turning instinctively towards the thickest part of the wood.

The Foreign Office, as she expected, was surrounded by a thick belt of officialdom, and Clara slackened her pace, as she approached it. You see, it was so very shady and mysterious. She felt too frightened just then to try and penetrate far into its obscurity, and so sat down under a tree.

Suddenly she noticed a small insect bobbing up and down incessantly in a sort of rut, and being devoted to natural history, and not at all alarmed, she ran up to see what it was.

It was an insignificant thing, though with a ludicrously self-satisfied air. There it remained in the same rut, proudly rocking itself to and fro, and making no headway. It had a large wooden head, and some awkward flappers on its back, which it waggled about continually; but its whole appearance was so strange that Clara could not decide whether it was animal, vegetable, or mineral.

"What are you?" asked Clara. "Are you in pain? You *are* a curious looking creature."

"I am the Rocking-Horse Fly," said the creature, looking up, and continuing its foolish exercise, until Clara felt quite sea-sick.

"And why are you called that?" asked Clara. "You don't look as if you could fly."

"Ah! But I can though," answered the Insect, proudly. "You should just see me flying in the face of Providence; why, I'm at it all the time."

"What funny legs you have got!"

"Yes, you see I'm supported by large screws and cranks; the one's useful, and the other's ornamental."

"Are there many more beautiful flies like you in the world?"

"No!" said it, with great dignity. "I am essentially one-horse."

"You seem to be badly bunkered just now; can I help you out?" asked Clara, kindly.

"No, my dear, you are not nearly strong enough to do that. Besides, I am used to my groove. In fact, I revel in it."

As Clara saw that it would be useless to try and help the foolish creature, and as her spirits were adapting themselves to the surrounding gloom, she made her way, without further hesitation, to the Foreign Office itself.

Again Clara's courage began to forsake her when she found herself gazing at this fine architectural pile. "What a lot of room there must be in a place like that—for improvement," she said to herself.

At the door was standing a very handsome footman, who was busily engaged in twiddling his thumbs.

He glanced at Clara, superciliously, but not unkindly. "Qu'est-ce que vous voulez, mademoiselle?" said he, shrugging his shoulders gracefully.

"Oh!" said Clara, "Why does he speak like that?"

"You are Ingleesh, mees. What for you come here?"

"I want to see Mr Downing, or somebody, and give him this letter."

"You ca'n't do that," said the flunky. "This is the Foreign Office." And he showed her a card on which was printed:—

"Now you'll understand," he said, "why it's called the Foreign Office. You see, if you'd been a foreigner, Mr Downing might have seen you, and he might have given you something nice. Master's so kind to foreigners, particularly Germans. He's fond of feeding them on slices of British Empire."

Clara wondered why she had not thought of this before she came, and was so impressed by the good sense of the footman's remarks that she handed him the letter without a word, and walked sadly away.

Flamjingos

"Now it's no use," said the Red Queen, who seemed to have sprung up out of the ground, and stood right in front of Clara. "It's no use your bothering about *that* sort of thing. You ca'n't change our established institutions, and you'll never get on in Blunderland until you have learnt that. Bless you, child, years and years ago I thought there were lots of things I could improve, and I used to talk of 'Reform' and all that rubbish; but, mark my words, you must take things as you find 'em, if you want to be happy here.

"Now, don't argue with me," she said to Clara, who had been standing with her hands behind her back, not even trying to get a word in edgeways. "Don't argue with me. Come and see the Demonstration."

She had hardly spoken when a cry was raised of "The Procession's coming," and a most brilliant and exclusive company began to stream into view. The Red Queen at once took the lead. "You see," she said, to Clara, "if I don't somebody else will, and then the muddle would be awful."

The Duchess was there, looking crosser than ever, and trembling all over whenever her eye caught the Queen's. The Welsh Rabbit was sniffing suspiciously at a leek which they'd offered to him, but as he'd eaten a large one at Birmingham, he said he never took them now unless they were forced upon him. Then there was the White Rabbit in a new wig, the March Hare and the Hatter, and the Cat. And there, right in the background, propped up somehow on his wall again, was poor old Crumpty-Bumpty. He looked very, dismal, and seemed quite out of shape, and when Clara came closer to him, she found that he was quite cracked about the Hyphen, and only held together by extracts from the *Star* and the *Daily News*.

"How dare you go near that creature?" said the Red Queen, angrily, to Clara. "Come away at once."

"I only looked super—super—ciliously at her, when she talked to me like that," explained Clara, to Geraldine afterwards.

After a painful pause the Red Queen said to Clara, "Child, come and be a muddied oaf." Clara only curtseyed, and joined the Procession, though as a matter of fact, she really didn't know the difference between that and a flannelled fool.

"It's only her fun, you know," Clara found the Duchess whispering in her ear. "We're not really going to play with all these people, my nerves wouldn't stand it. We're going to watch the Flamjingos play."

"Who are the Flamjingos?" asked Clara. "I don't think I ever heard of them before."

"Well," replied the Duchess, "nobody seems quite to know, but they're very useful creatures, when they don't get *too* excited, and it's very pretty to watch them at play. *She*," pointing with her chin at the Red Queen as she spoke, "would like to join in the game herself, but we restrain her."

"I wonder how you do it," said Clara.

"Hush, my dear," the Duchess whispered. "Some subjects are too sacred to be talked about, and that's one of them."

As she spoke the Procession entered a large open space in which, to her great delight, Clara saw hundreds upon hundreds of Flamjingos running about, and cackling as loudly as ever they could.

They certainly were the most curious birds she had ever seen and were even more peculiar, though not of course so repulsive, as the strange creatures she had left behind her in Boerdom. They were painting everything red when Clara came up, and each had a tin trumpet in its hand, and, tied to the feathers of its tail, a small Union Jack, which it continually waggled in the breeze. When they all blew and waggled together—which they did every three minutes—the effect was indescribable, and Clara felt as though she must choke with the patriotic feelings which the magnificent spectacle aroused in her breast. At the same time they all sang different songs, such as "*Rule Britannia*", "*Soldiers of the Queen*", "*The Absent-Minded Beggar*", and "*The British Navy*", and as none of them knew *all* the words of any of the songs, and sang what they did know to tunes which they invented as they went on, you will understand that the noise was deafening.

For a long time Clara could not make out what they were playing at, but at last she found out that it was a kind of football, in which the balls were things like hedgehogs, which every now and then came out of holes in the ground in which they lay concealed. These creatures turned out to be really Slinky Pros, which had left their garden to try and get other creatures to come and live with them in Boerdom. Whenever one of these showed itself, which, being very persistent beasts, happened every now and then, all the Flamjingos who caught sight of it immediately rushed at it, and tried to kick it to the other end of the ground. As far as Clara could make out, the game consisted in the Slinky Pros trying to meet, and the Flamjingos trying to prevent them. Whenever two of them managed to keep together for three seconds, that scored one to them, and when the Flamjingos kicked them apart before this happened, they marked ten points, and sang as much of the National Anthem as they could remember on the spur of the moment.

The Pros didn't seem to like the game at all, and one or two of them, who had had the spines rubbed off their backs by all the pushing and kicking they went through, threatened to tell *Truth*. And one very slinky one indeed only managed to escape being kicked to death by disguising himself as an honest policeman. Nobody, however, seemed to think the behaviour of one or the other at all extraordinary, since, as the Red Queen very appropriately put it, this was "a place where girt with friends or foes a man might speak the thing he would, and clump over the head anybody who spoke the thing he wouldn't."

Clara couldn't feel very much pity for the Pros, for they seemed such dirty little creatures, and she noticed that whenever two of them *did* manage to meet they always began to explain to one another what wicked people their relations were, and how their brothers revelled in atrocities of the most awful kind.

She paid very little more attention to them, saying to herself, that it didn't matter very much after all if the Flamjingos did kick them to death, though she didn't quite like to see them doing it. So, like the others, she shut her eyes to it.

"What do you think of the game?" asked the Duchess, rather anxiously.

"Well," said Clara, "I'm afraid I don't quite follow it. It's very muddly up, I think."

"You see," said the Red Queen, decisively, "it suffers, like all football at the present day, from too much of the Pro element."

The strength of the Flamjingos appeared to be extraordinary, and Clara, who always took great interest in questions of eating and drinking, asked the Red Queen what they fed on.

"Declarations of war, my dear," answered the Queen, "and Regrettable Incidents."

"It must be rather an expensive sort of food," said Clara, thoughtfully.

"You may say that, child," said the Red Queen, "but it doesn't matter very much. The Duchess has to pay for them; I don't. And the Pros, as you know, belong to Crumpty-Bumpty."

All this time the Dalmeny Cat kept appearing and disappearing in the air, until at last the Red Queen noticed it and said in a very decided voice, "That Cat must be destroyed."

"Why?" asked Clara, "I'm sure it's a very pretty Cat, and I don't see that it is doing any harm. It's not as though it were a real Cat, you know."

"I *don't* know," retorted the Queen, "but I *do* know that I am going to call the executioner and have its head chopped off at once."

"You ca'n't," said Clara, "it hasn't got body enough for that."

When the executioner, who turned out to be the Duchess in disguise, came up, there was the most tremendous row. She couldn't hit the head of the Cat, who disappeared whenever she struck at it, and then turned up again in a fresh place while part of the crowd cheered her efforts and the rest said, "Shame, Shame," until she was more nervous than ever.

At last the hubbub and confuslon grew so great that Clara thought she would never get out of it alive, and she said afterwards that she was sure she would never have escaped if it hadn't been for the Red Queen, who said, in the kindest way, "Just watch me, my dear, and do as I do."

With that the Queen and the Duchess each caught a Flamjingo, and got upon its back, and Clara after a good deal of trouble did the same. It was dreadfully uncomfortable on the Flamjingo's back, and Clara couldn't help feeling that she looked very ridiculous, but still there seemed to be no other way of escape, so she clung on, and the Flamjingos soon carried all three out of danger.

"I told you," said the Duchess, with a soft sleepy chuckle, as she hung on to the Flamjingo's neck, "that sometimes they are very useful birds."

CHAPTER X

Queens and Questions

*C*lara could never remember afterwards whether they left the Flamjingos or the Flamjingos left them; all she knew was that after riding for a long, long way through a great deal of mud, which splashed her frock most dreadfully, she found herself with a sort of crown on her head sitting between the Red Queen and the Duchess, who appeared to be very much out of temper with one another.

"You may say what you like," the Duchess was saying, in a discontented voice, "but I shall never get used to that kind of thing. We needn't have ridden those birds half so hard as we did. It's not respectable, and at my time of life I don't like it."

"Of course you don't," retorted the Red Queen, turning up her nose as she spoke. "You've never known how to move with the times."

"It's not at all necessary," said the Duchess, with conviction. "The *Times* always moves with me, except—except in China."

"If it hadn't been for me, I don't know what would have happened to you."

"Lots of things have happened to me that I don't like," said the poor Duchess, "and, do you know? I sometimes feel as if you were one of them, but," she went on, hastily, "don't suppose that I'm not grateful, your Majesty, but you *do* hustle me so, and it's not good for me. You know I lost my nerve ever so long ago. I wish you'd let Clara take my place."

"If she'll always do exactly what I tell her, I don't mind," said the Queen, "but she must pass the proper examination first."

"I didn't know one had to be examined for the higher offices," said Clara, very much surprised, "I thought it was only for the really important ones—the permanent ones I mean, you know."

"That," answered the Queen, "shows how little you know of the Cabinet System. Why we're always examining one another here. She," pointing at the Duchess, "has been plucked three times already, but we keep her on because she's very quiet and harmless now, and she's *so* respectable."

The poor Duchess could only wave her hands feebly in protest, and the Queen went on, "I proceed with the examination. Take his pay from a Yeoman and what remains?

Don't answer hurriedly—it's a departmental question, remember—and don't forget to say 'your Majesty'."

Clara thought for a long while, and at last she said, "Please, your Majesty, I'm not quite sure. The pay couldn't remain if it were taken away, and I shouldn't think the Yeoman would remain if he were not paid."

"So you think nothing would remain, do you?"

"Yes," answered Clara, thoughtfully, "I think that must be the answer."

"Wrong," said the Red Queen, "the Yeoman *would* remain. He always does, and you may thank your lucky stars it is so."

And the Duchess said, "Really, Clara, I'm surprised at you. Any corporal could have told you that."

Clara didn't feel at all comfortable at the way they spoke to her, but she was afraid to cry before the Red Queen, and resolved to do better next time.

"If," asked the Duchess, "you were really a queen—which you aren't yet, you know—and somebody like her Red Majesty kept pushing you into all sorts of places you didn't like, and making you say all sorts of things you didn't really mean, what would you do?"

"I don't know, I'm sure," said Clara, "but I think I should run away."

"I only wish *I* could," answered the poor Duchess, with tears in her eyes, "but," looking sulkily at the Queen, "if she were too fast for you, you couldn't. But," sighing gently, "that wasn't an examination question, you know. I only asked for information."

"Your grace is a great deal too fond of information of that sort," growled the Queen. "You'll be getting some that's unauthentic and therefore inaccurate, if you don't take care."

The Duchess turned pale. "You needn't bring up things like that," she said, "or I shall begin to talk about three acres and a cow. So there!"

After this they were both silent for some time, during which each seemed to be thinking of something very unpleasant, but at last the Queen said, in a milder tone, "What's your way of keeping a House clean?"

"To stay away from it as much as ever I can," answered Clara, promptly, for she felt sure she was right this time.

"Quite right, my dear," said the Duchess, eagerly. "That's just what I always say. Nobody sees the dust if you don't stir it up. And, if you must go indoors, keep in bed as much as possible."

"It's not a bit right," complained the Queen. "The proper way is to call the servants all the names you can think of. I'm afraid you're totally unfitted for domestic legislation."

"I'll do my best," said Clara, humbly, "if you'll only teach me."

"That's a good child," said the Queen, kindly. "Come to me whenever you're in a difficulty and I'll either get you out or—"

"Or what, your Majesty?" asked Clara.

"Or get you deeper in, of course," answered the Red Queen. "Really you are very dull."

Clara didn't know quite what to say to this kind offer so she only curtseyed and laid her crown at the Queen's feet.

"There, there, child," said the Queen, impatiently. "Put it on again. You don't suppose it's a real one, do you? If you want it to shine at all you will have to manage to keep close to me, and then it may catch a little reflected glory from mine."

"What a very disagreeable creature she is," thought Clara, to herself, and she was just going to declare that she would have nothing more to do with her, when the Queen said, in a very peremptory tone:—

"Where's your programme?"

"If you please, your Majesty," said Clara, hastily, "they didn't give me one."

"Rubbish," retorted the Queen. "Why, there are any amount of old ones lying about all over the place. You should have picked one up."

"But wouldn't that be stealing?" asked Clara, who was a very honest little girl.

"Certainly not," answered the Queen. "They're mostly unauthorized, and the others are discarded. Anybody's free to pick 'em up. You can have one of my old ones, if you like."

"Thank you very much indeed," said Clara, "but it ca'n't be much use, I'm afraid, if it doesn't say what you are really going to do."

"Tut, tut, child, you don't understand. Programmes *never* tell what's going to happen. They only tell what's *not* going to happen, and there's such a lot of that it doesn't much matter what's on them so long as they keep clear of facts."

"Dear me," said Clara, "do you know, I never saw it in that light before, but of course I understand now. I think I should like one of the Duchess's, if I might," she added.

"I lost mine years and years ago," whimpered the poor Duchess. "I'm sure you're quite welcome to it if you can find it, but I've forgotten what it was all about. I know there was something to do with a turkey and a bear in it, but I backed the wrong horse just about that time, and I've never been able to remember things properly since."

"You'll have to take one of mine, only not that which says I was a Home Ruler before Gladstone. You'd better tear that up quietly if you come across it. There are lots of others to choose from," said the Queen. "You ca'n't go about looking ridiculous without one, and I can let you have one all in words of one syllable. Then you'll be *quite* happy."

"Couldn't I make up one of my very own?" asked Clara, eagerly. "You mayn't believe it, but I can write quite nicely, and it would be such fun."

"You dare to do anything of the kind," screamed the Red Queen, in a great passion, "and I'll have you superseded before you know where you are."

"I only wish I did know where I was," said poor little Clara.

"Come along, my dear, I'll show you," said the Duchess, kindly. "Come along with me. You mustn't mind her."

C H A P T E R **XI**

Dragon and Turnturtle

"Y̶ou haven't got a mission, have you?" said the Duchess to Clara, rather anxiously.

"Certainly not," Clara replied, in great surprise. "I've always been taught that it's most vulgar to have anything of the kind. I don't think," she added, thoughtfully, "I should even know a Cassowary if I met one."

"Ah!" said the Duchess, in a tone of great relief. "Then I can take you to see the Dragon and the Turnturtle. They're both perfectly tame, except the Dragon. He goes mad whenever he sees a missionary. I should like you to see how ready they are to eat out of my hand."

"Did you tame them?" asked Clara.

"Well, yes, so the papers say, my dear," answered the Duchess, blushing a little.

"Do they come to you, when you call them?"

"Well, not exactly, they never did that, and I don't suppose they ever will. You see, my method has always been to be very gentle with them. And now they're so docile that I can make them do just what they like," said the Duchess, triumphantly. "Come and look at them."

So Clara and the Duchess left the Red Queen (who said she wanted to come and stir the Turnturtle up with a long spoon, and hear him quote texts, but was persuaded to remain behind), and made their way along Imperial Road, at the extreme end of which the Duchess said the two animals lived.

After some time they came in sight of the two creatures sitting on the ground and telling one another sad stories of the deaths of kings. They received the Duchess very politely, though Clara could not help thinking there was a scornful glint in the Dragon's eye whenever he looked at her, and the Turnturtle muttered something about wishing the Duchess was the Dalmeny Cat.

However, they both seemed very relieved when they learned that the Red Queen had been left behind.

"A nasty, spiteful thing," the Turnturtle called her, while the Dragon said he had never had the pleasure of meeting her, but understood she had no feelings, and fewer manners.

"You may thank your lucky stars you've never had anything to do with the Red Queen," said the Turnturtle.

"I ca'n't stop, myself," said the Duchess, after Clara had timidly taken each of the great creatures by the paw, "because it's spring cleaning in the House, and I've got to shift some heavy responsibilities, but the young lady has come because she wanted to hear your histories, and I couldn't tell her much about you. I hope you'll tell them as truly as you can."

"That's not saying much," muttered the Dragon, aside, but he only said out loud, "Delighted, I'm sure, Shall I begin, Turtle, or will you?"

"Oh, *you*," replied the Turnturtle. "Mine's so sad, and besides I've got a sermon to prepare on brotherly love, with an excursus on the proper treatment of our black brother, and I can be thinking it out while you're talking."

"Once," said the Dragon, "I was a real Dragon." And then he remained silent for so long, looking at his damaged claws, that Clara was very nearly thanking him for his story, and asking the Turnturtle for his.

However, after signing several queer looking documents with a red pencil, the Dragon seemed to recover himself, and he went on, "But now, as you see, I'm only paper, and they say I shall soon have to be cut up into little bits and used for Christmas decorations."

"You'll leave me a slice in your will, wo'n't you?" said Clara, eagerly. "I should so like to take it home. It would be quite a diplomatic triumph."

"You shouldn't use such long words," said the Dragon. "I'm sure you don't know the meaning of the word diplomacy. Nobody does where *you* come from."

"There was a time," continued the Dragon, mournfully, "when you might have had as many slices as you liked, but I've made other arrangements now. If I've got to be cut up, I may as well get the best terms I can, and I know a party—an overbearing sort of chap he is too—who'll keep the dissectors away from me for ever so long on condition he has my head when they *do* begin."

"But wouldn't the Duchess protect you?" asked Clara, in surprise.

Both creatures burst into a roar of laughter.

"*She* protect me!" cried the Dragon.

"Why," bellowed the Turnturtle, "she ca'n't even protect herself against a simple rustic person like me. You've only to roar at her and she runs away at once."

"You surprise me," said Clara. "I always understood she had such a resolute disposition."

The Dragon grinned. "Ask her about Port Arthur," he said.

"And Venezuela," said the Turnturtle.

"You see," said the Dragon, "she never went to a really good school like we did."

"I've been to a good school too," said Clara, "if it comes to that."

"What did they teach you there?" inquired the Turnturtle, anxiously.

"Reading, Writing, and Arithmetic," replied Clara, "but I'm afraid I was never much good at the last."

"At ours," said the Dragon, "they taught us Bleeding and Blighting, thoroughly."

"And," said the Turnturtle, "I was taught Mathematics—Sedition, Abstraction, Stultification, and Provision."

"What's the use of Provision?" asked Clara.

"To teach you how to provide for yourself, of course," said the Turnturtle. "I mastered *that* rule."

"But didn't they teach you any real sums like the Rule-of-Three?" asked Clara.

"No," replied the Turnturtle, scornfully. "I worked that out for myself, and the answer was, 'Steyn, Schreiner, and ME'."

The Dragon, who didn't seem to care much for questions of modern education, said abruptly to the Turnturtle: "That professional spouter of yours, Doctor Leyds, wasn't exactly a topside success, was he? Clever young fellow, too. Nice, gentleman-like manners, good address. Christian, too, I understand?"

"They imposed upon him," snapped the Turnturtle; "and he, poor fellow, without knowing it, I'm sure, imposed upon me."

The Dragon rolled with laughter. "I nearly died of suffocation," he said, "when I saw in the papers that you expected France and Germany to fight your battles. Why, my dear fellow, it was a monstrous thing. They ca'n't even afford to fight each other!"

"Leyds did his best," sighed the Turnturtle. "But what makes it so bitter is the money it cost. Why, we've been keeping the editorial staffs of Continental newspapers for the last ten years." And then, spreading out his fins in despair, he broke into the following dirge:—

"Will you join our little gamble?" said the Doctor to the Gauls,
"There'll be heaps of pretty pickings when the monster Britain
falls;
See how Christianlike the journalists of Christian Paris write!
Since we've paid them to shout 'Kroojer'; will you come and join
the fight?
Will you, wo'n't you, will you, wo'n't you, will you join the
fight?
Will you, wo'n't you, will you, wo'n't you, wo'n't you join
the fight?"

"You can really have no notion how your commerce will get on,
We can go for Sam together, when we've kicked the life from
John;"
But the Gaul replied, "My hands are full," and shut his pocket
tight,
Said he thanked the Doctor kindly, but he would not join the
fight.
Would not, could not, would not, could not, would not join
the fight,
Would not, could not, would not, could not, could not join
the fight.

"O think of the religious life!" the wily Boer replied,
"While Britain's here we cannot tan the Kaffir's heathen hide;
The further off is England the more we can unite,
To sweat the blacks, with lash and tax, so come and join the
*   fight!*
*   Will you, wo'n't you, will you, wo'n't you, will you join the*
*   fight?*
*   Will you, wo'n't you, will you, wo'n't you, wo'n't you join*
*   the fight?"*

When the Turnturtle broke off, sobbing unconstrainedly, the Dragon turned to Clara, and solemnly winked his eye.

"You know better than that, don't you?" he asked. "Now, just oblige me, little girl, by standing up, hands behind your back, and repeating, *'Tis the voice of the Sluggard'*. It will do our friend here a world of good. Begin firmly, and grow feeble as you go on."

Clara was so used to being ordered about by this time that she never thought of refusing this request, and standing up immediately, she recited the well-known poem, in the following fashion:—

'Tis the voice of Aunt Sarum—"You'd better take care,
If you do that again I shall ruffle your hair."
As the sand to an Ostrich, so words are to her,
She can bury herself in a threat, and not stir,
When the foe's giving in, she's as fierce as a Dragon,
She will pull of his clothes till he hasn't a rag on;
But when he says "NO!" and stamps hard on the ground,
Her voice has a timid and tremulous sound.

"The next verse," said the Dragon. "It begins with, *'I passed by his garden'*." Go ahead."

And Clara went on:—

I looked in at China and marked without fright,
How the Bear and the Froggy were putting things right;
The Froggy got promises splendid and grand
While the Bear was content with a bird in the hand;
When the bargain was over, the Bear, rather blown,
With great condescension accepted a loan,
While the Froggy received only papers and seals,
And concluded the business by kic—"

"What *is* the use of repeating all that stuff?" interrupted the Turnturtle. "It doesn't contain one word about independence! Pure balderdash!"

"Yes, I think you'd better leave off," said the Dragon, uneasily. "I didn't at all like your reference to the Bear, though your omission of England from the conclusion of the bargain was remarkably fine—remarkably. Quite masterly!"

"England!" cried the Turnturtle. "The name is poison to me! And oh, I used to think that it was poison to everybody else, and I thought I had only to say, 'Down with England', and all the rest of the world would flock sword in hand to South Africa."

"Well, so they did, some of them," answered Clara. "There were the Australians and Canadians, and contingents from India and Ceylon. Did you want any more?"

"Not of that sort," sighed the Turnturtle. "And they came mounted!"

Clara grew a little red. "They're still a little uncivilized in those parts," she said, apologetically, "and we tried to stop them, you know."

"Come, come," cried the Dragon, "you two are enough to give anybody a fit of the dumps. Cheer up, cheer up!" And digging the Turnturtle in the place where most people's ribs grow, the Dragon implored the old creature to sing something really bright and catchy. "Sing that jolly little thing you and Steyn composed about two years ago," he said.

"It's a duet," objected the Turnturtle, "and there's no one now to take Steyn's part."

"Oh, I'll do that," laughed the Dragon. "I don't mind facing the music for him—not in the least. Now then, One!—two!—three!"

And they sang as follows:—

Beautiful war so pure and right,
Christian Burghers love a fight,
Europe, of coarse, will join the Boer,
War against England, Beautiful war!
War against England, Beautiful war!
  Beau—ootiful Wa—ar!
  Beau—ootiful Wa—ar!
Wa–ar against Eng—Eng—land,
  Beautiful, Beautiful War!

Beautiful War! The Boers are 'cute,
White is the flag 'neath which they shoot,
Break their oath, and sing hymns before
Potting an ambulance—beautiful War!
  Beau—ootiful Wa—ar!
  Beau—ootiful Wa—ar!
Wa—ar against Eng—Eng—land,
  Beautiful, Beauti—FUL WAR!

"Chorus again!" cried the Dragon, who was laughing consumedly, but the Turnturtle burst into such a flow of tears that Clara, who was really very tender-hearted, and who feared she might be tempted to give the Turtle anything he asked, took to her heels and ran with all her might to find the Red Queen.

"I feel rather faint," she thought, "and I want a little bolstering up."

CHAPTER **XII**

On the Cards

$\mathcal{B}$ut while Clara was running along to find the Red Queen she met the White Rabbit again, who shouted to her to stop.

"I've got 'em all here," he said, showing her piles and piles of stamped and addressed envelopes.

"All what?" asked Clara.

"Why these, don't you see they're the writs?"

"Then you ought to take them to the County Court at once," said Clara, who was a very clever little girl, and knew that respectable people were never seen with anything of the kind, except in Ireland.

"Oh, they're not that sort at all, Miss," said the Rabbit, very politely. "These are the writs inviting everybody to the great trial where there's no prisoner, and where pretty nearly all the company ought to be in the dock. I've got one for you among the rest."

"But I don't belong to the trial at all," complained Clara. "I'm what you call detached."

98

"Well you'll find you'd better come, whether or no," retorted the Rabbit. "I suppose you don't want to have the verdict go against you, do you?"

At this moment there was a great ringing of bells, and blowing of fog-horns, and, as everything seemed to be dissolving all round her, Clara ran as hard as she could to the big building which the Rabbit said was the Court-House.

When she got inside she found that the trial had already begun, and that everybody was accusing everybody else of all the crimes he could think of.

On the bench sat Britannia ("looking for all the world like a middle-aged mermaid without a tail," said Clara, afterwards). She seemed dreadfully confused by all the noise and bluster. She wore her helmet over her wig, and was trying very hard to look judicial, but it was quite plain that she could not make out in the least what all the dispute was about, and again and again implored somebody to tell her. By her side crouched a stuffed lion, with a much twisted tail, which roared mechanically when she dug it in the ribs. This she did, whenever she did not quite know what else to do.

"You see, I don't understand politics, and I don't know why they make me pretend that I care what happens," said Britannia, to Clara.

"You're evidently quite at sea here," piped the White King, in a squeaky voice, as he struggled hard to climb up the pinnacle of fame.

"At sea?" cried Britannia. "I wish I was at sea. The Flamjingos keep telling me I rule the waves, but I ca'n't rule a straight line in politics anyhow. Nobody can."

"I'll guide your hand, when I get up there," squeaked the White King, swarming up the pinnacle, as if he thought the lion was going to bite him.

He puffed and blew so hard that Clara picked him up between her finger and thumb, and placed him safely on the top of the wool-sack.

"You know," he said, looking round the Court, "I could have got up all by myself, if I'd liked."

The White King's notion of guiding Britannia's hand was to bellow advice into her ear, and he used such long words that poor Britannia got more confused than ever.

Of course, directly Clara entered the Court, she had tried to take her seat, but this was just what she was not allowed to do. The ushers explained to her that it was altogether illegal while the trial was going on, "unless, indeed," as one of them said, "nobody has anything to say against you, which," he rather rudely added, "I know isn't the case with you."

It was quite extraordinary to see what tremendous excitement the entrance of Clara's various acquaintances created. The March Hare and the Hatter, who came in fighting, and trying to strangle one another, were received with cheers and groans, and the Walrus and the Carpenter with groans and cheers. The Duchess, who tried to push a great many people in through a side door, was turned out again with extreme violence, and told to mind her own business, and the fitful appearances of the Dalmeny Cat were greeted with tempests of execration. Some of the people pretended to be very fond of the Cat, and called, "Puss! Puss!" but when it came close to them they abused it, and tried to hit it.

At last it became so disgusted that it threatened to vanish for good and all, and never come near the Court again; but it kept returning fitfully. At last Clara thought it had really gone; but, suddenly, she looked up, and there it was with Britannia and the White King on the platform.

"What are you doing up there?" asked Clara, surprised. "That's the place for the Judges."

"I know," said the Cat, "I have elected myself a judge of things in general. It's not so worrying." And the Court agreed to look upon it in that capacity for the future.

"What are all those oysters in that box for?" asked Clara, of the White Rabbit, "and why do they keep writing crosses on bits of paper?"

"Those are the people that ran away from the Walrus and the Carpenter. They're the jury, who have to come to decisions, and they make those marks to show that they are all at cross purposes and don't know their own minds."

The noise was so great that it was all the White Rabbit could do to make himself heard. He shouted, "Order! Order!" continually, and at last he said to Britannia, almost crossly, "I do wish you wouldn't make that lion roar so."

When the tumult had a little subsided Crumpty-Bumpty, who was heavily fettered by prejudice, managed somehow to attract the attention of the jury, and demanded to be allowed to give his evidence.

"But," said poor Britannia, "there isn't anybody to give evidence against, and I'm sure I don't know what you're all talking about."

"You just wait, Mum," shouted Crumpty-Bumpty, "till you've heard what I've got to say against Clara there. She'll be in the dock in two two's, if only you'll listen to me." And without waiting for permission, he immediately began:—

They told me what I had to do
Could easily be done:—
"You've got to split yourself in Two,
And say you feel like One."

They said, I'd got to keep my head,
And keep a valiant heart,
And keep (the very words thy said)
The heads and tails apart.

She gave the Voters This and That,
She gave them Black and White,
She gave them Tit, she gave them Tat,
She gave them Left and Right.

I said "The Boers have got to live,
I'll give them place and sway,
And when I've nothing else to give,
I'll gave myself away."

MY notion was to hunt with Perks,
And run with Labouchere;
But she maintains that only works
When Lloyd-George isn't there.

Don't let them think I want to lead,
For what I want to be
Must ever be a secret creed,
Between myself and me.

When Crumpty-Bumpty had finished, there was a dead silence for a minute or two, and then the March Hare suddenly began to scream, "Suppress that Clara! Behead that Clara! Put that Clara in Kilmainham, and cut her hair short!" and was led out foaming at the mouth.

"What a very disagreeable person!" thought Clara, to herself. "I wonder if he's always like that."

"You will please," said Britannia, in a solemn voice, "address yourself to the very serious charges brought against you by the last witness. The March Hare's remarks may be disregarded—the Court is perfectly acquainted with his somewhat perfervid temperament—but to the evidence of Crumpty-Bumpty you must offer some reply or suffer the extreme penalty of the law."

While Clara was racking her brains to think of something to say in answer to Crumpty-Bumpty, she was conscious of a most curious sensation as though she was getting bigger and bigger every minute. For some time past she had felt a great deal too big for her boots, and had grown accustomed to the feeling, but this was something quite different. She appeared to herself to be getting too big for the Court altogether, and even Britannia appeared quite a tiny little figure, when she compared her with herself.

"If you go on swelling like that," said the Red Queen, who was standing beside her, and who had done nothing but shout "Traitor" since the trial began, "there wo'n't be room for two of us in the same room. Disgraceful, I call it."

"I ca'n't help it," pleaded poor Clara, "one must develop, you know."

"Nobody ever developed quicker than I did," retorted the Red Queen, in a very sulky tone. "But there's reason in all things, and if you're going to grow into a giantess before my very eyes, you may manage Crumpty-Bumpty for yourself."

"Please stay and help me," implored Clara, "I ca'n't think what to say, and I am depending on you." But all the time she kept on feeling herself growing stronger, and bigger, and bigger, and stronger, until she said to herself, "I don't care if she does go. Half the creatures here are make-believe, and the rest pasteboard. Why I believe they're only a pack of rubbish after all."

"Pack," cried the Red Queen. "Well, what do you expect at a political meeting? We have to pack them all at the present day."

Then everything became confused and all sense of proportion was lost. The furniture began to move about, and the building rocked to its foundations. People who were seated found themselves suddenly out in the cold, and people who were standing were unexpectedly hustled into most uncomfortable seats. Everything trembled in the balance. Above the confusion rose cries of "Bribery", "Corruption", "Lies", and all sorts of creatures crowded upon poor Clara until she cried out for her Aunt Sarum to take her home.

But the more she cried the more they all hustled her, until at last all the creatures rose in the air and came flying in her face.

"Why, I do believe," said Clara, "that you're nothing but a lot of pictures. There's nothing in you after all."

But Clara was mistaken, for when they fell face downwards Clara saw that on their backs were the most dreadful legends, such as:—

"CITY OF LONDON—TWO ANTI-VACCINATIONISTS,
SEVEN VEGETARIANS, AND AN ANTI-GAMBLER";

"KENT—SEVEN TEETOTALERS,
AND A DECEASED WIFE'S SISTER";

"BIRMINGHAM—FOUR SOCIALISTS,
TWO PECULIAR PEOPLE, AND A FIELD CORNET",

and things like that. She closed her eyes so as not to read the writing upon them, but they only came thicker and thicker, and faster and faster until—

Clara thought she had better wake up.

And it was time.

Lightning Source UK Ltd.
Milton Keynes UK
12 June 2010
155498UK00001B/34/P